# THAILAND'S MOVIE THEATRES
## RELICS, RUINS AND THE ROMANCE OF ESCAPE

ฮอลลีวู้ด

HOLLYWOOD

10

NEW ODEON
UNITED KRUNG ODHON CO. LTD.
นิวโอเดียน
บริษัท สหกรณ์ชน จำกัด
新高亭戲院

This Pass is not Exempted from
Revenue Tax

009737

NEW ODEON

ศาลาเฉลิมกรุง

เลขที่ 550764

12.50
BAHT

12.50
BAHT
พาราเมาท์
12.50

Paramount
Pictures

เลขที่ 3724

ชั้นล่าง  DOWNSTAIRS

No 00047

นิวโอเดียน

THIS PASS IS NOT EXEMPTED FROM REVENUE TAX

NEW ODEON

TEL. 32184 - 32563
UNITED KRUNG ODHON CO. LTD.

16.00       15.00

BAHT       บาท

คาเธ่ย์
CATHAY

เล่มที่
ตั๋วเข้าชมมหรสพ โรงภาพยนตร์       No 38509

บางปะอินรามา

ศูนย์การค้า บ.ข.ส. อำเภอบางปะอิน จังหวัดอยุธยา
หมายเลขทะเบียนมหรสพ

วันที่       เดือน       พ.ศ.

ราคา 15 บาท       เลขที่นั่ง

เลขที่  8584

บัตรชมภาพยนตร์

12.50 บาท

เน่าๆ

อมรา-งามตา-สิทน
และ อาลม มารนนห์
ที่.....เริ่มใหร่

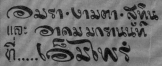

บัตรชมภาพยนตร์       No. 0308

โรงภาพยนตร์
เฉลิม ป.

เลขที่ 37 ถนนเทศบาล 15 หลังสถานีรถไฟ
อำเภอปากช่อง จังหวัดนครราชสีมา

ราคา 30.-

12.50

9156

QUEEN'S       ควีนส์

7
BAHT       ขอได้รับความขอบพระคุณมาก

ศาลาเฉลิมไทย

07457

16.45น.

CHALERM THAI

10
BAHT       พระโขนงเธียเตอร์       บาท

93558

รวม อ.ม.ภ.ท.

13.30

PRAKANONG THEATRE

80       8

เล่มที่  060       สยาม       เล่มที่  060

สยามสแควร์ กรุงเทพมหานคร

No  5999       No  5999

ค่าชมภาพยนตร์ ราคา 80 บาท       ค่าชมภาพยนตร์ ราคา 80 บาท

ส่วนของผู้ชม       ส่วนของเจ้าหน้าที่

เลขที่  67747       เล่มที่  678       เลขที่  67747

โรงภาพยนตร์
แสกาลาแ

ทะเบียนการค้าเลขที่ 82 49 0615

765/156 หมู่ที่ 3 ต.ท่าข้าม อ.พุนพิน จ.สุราษฎร์ธานี

วันที่

รอบ       น.

ราคา 10 บาท

ทะเบียนการค้าเลขที่
82 49 0615

โรงภาพยนตร์ สุทัศน์

765/156 หมู่ที่ 3 ต.ท่าข้าม อ.พุนพิน จ.สุราษฎร์ธานี

ราคา
10
บาท       วันที่

รอบ

เลขที่นั่ง

*To my late uncle Morton Winston,*
*without whom I may have never known*
*Thailand or its movie theatres.*

First published in Thailand in 2019 by
River Books Co., Ltd.
396 Maharaj Road, Tatien, Bangkok 10200
Tel: 66 2 225 4963 | 66 2 224 6686
E-mail: order@riverbooksbk.com
www.riverbooksbk.com

Editor: Sarah Rooney
Design: Ruetairat Nanta
Production: Paisarn Piemmettawat
Publisher: Narisa Chakrabongse

ISBN 978 616 451 023 4

Front cover: Fah Siam theatre, Suphanburi
Back cover: Scala theatre, Bangkok
Page 3: Wik Kru Thawee theatre, Ratchaburi province
Opposite: Projector at the Luna theatre, Yala

Printed and bound in Thailand
by Sirivatana Interprint Public Co., Ltd.

# CONTENTS

# PREFACE

We have heard the analogies.

To the devout, the movie theatre is a temple, a holy sermon hall where the congregation prays for transcendence. To the sensuous, it is a gladiatorial arena, loud and unholy, where the crowd cheers and laughs and claps and sobs at the spectacle. And to the surrealist, the cinema is a coffin, a very large coffin, dark except for the screen, sealed off and removed from reality, a collective coffin where the dead dream of heaven and the living dream of light.

Lately, movie theatres – the standalone structures photographed in their glorious dereliction in this book – have become something else for almost everyone in Thailand: nostalgia. Or worse, a fading memory, a sepia album slowly disintegrating in an age where worshippers pray to the moving-image deities, not in the collective blackness of cinemas but in private – at home, on their little personal screens – or in artificially bright, neon-smeared multiplexes that value plasticity over elegance. The coffin metaphor becomes an ironic self-prophecy, for the graveyard of architecture is now stacked with the ruins of standalone cinemas, the rubble of marquees, discarded chandeliers and defaced facades, as old movie temples have been replaced by mega-malls, parking garages and high-rise condos.

Empire, King, Queen, Prince, Krung Kasem, Mackenna, Colesium, Paramount, Hollywood, Athens, Siam Theatre, Lido – the movie houses of those glorious days are now just names and reminiscences. In Bangkok, only the Scala remains as the last standalone cinema (standing alone, it is) and no one knows for how much longer. The disappearance of these grand dames, which flaunted palatial, art-deco, cubist, and a mongrel of mid-century design, provokes more than just a bitter nostalgia: it's proof of a monumental shift, for better or worse, in our economic behaviour and consumerist impulses. We used to *go to the movies*; now we *go to malls* that happen to have movie screens in them. To some, it doesn't matter. To others, it does: film was the art that shaped the consciousness of the 20th century, and the way we experienced it also shaped our childhood, our memories, our worldview and our social interaction.

If that sounds like a naive ode to what is forever lost, then perhaps it is. If that sounds like romantic Marxism – come on, those ageing standalone theatres were no longer economically viable in capitalistic Thailand! – then I stand before the firing squad with my chest puffed up in pride, because one of my earliest cinematic memories was when my parents took me to watch *King Kong* (the Jessica Lange version, the original posters of which can be seen on pages 186 and 187) in that big, dark place – not like a coffin, but like a strange dream made up of atomised light – and since then there has been an odd pull that has compelled me to keep going back for more.

I suspect that's what Philip Jablon felt, too, when he trekked through the necropolis of forgotten movie houses to capture their splendid dereliction. He can't resurrect the dead, no more than anyone can relive the golden era of standalone cinemas in Thailand. The temple has fallen and the coffin nailed. But at least on these pages their memory will not fade, their light will not be extinguished, and the congregation of worshippers, haunted by the dream of atomised light, will continue to pray.

Kong Rithdee
April 2019

Ticket collector at the Nakhon Non Rama theatre,
Pracharat Road, Nonthaburi.

# INTRODUCTION

I don't really remember what caused me to make a wrong turn down that hitherto unknown street in Chiang Mai back in November 2007. Simple curiosity, I guess. Wanderlust, maybe. From the corner of my eye I glimpsed a rust-streaked movie marquee perched above the road. The sight of it piqued my curiosity, leading me to stray even further from my original destination. A quick turn off the main road brought me into a steamy wet market, at the far end of which stood the Tippanetr theatre, then one of the city's last standalone movie theatres.

Prior to that, I hadn't given much thought to the legacy of movie-going in Chiang Mai. I naively figured that movie theatres had come with the development of shopping malls, an assumption which precluded the 700-year-old city from ever having known the majesty of a downtown movie palace or the down-home intimacy of a neighbourhood theatre. But standing before me was an example of the former, its paint-chipped modernist facade overlooking a bustling bazaar in a gritty corner of town.

With the Tippanetr, a whole new facet of Chiang Mai's social history appeared before me; a world which – to my foreign eyes – seemed more authentic, more human than the plastic shopping mall multiplexes ever had. Indeed, the contrast between the two movie theatre worlds was stark. The multiplexes confined within shopping malls had always felt cheap and antiseptic; cutting edge as far as comfort and technology were concerned, but otherwise devoid of any character. The Tippanetr, on the other hand, even in all its faded grandeur, was the embodiment of character. I made a mental note to come back and catch a film at this ageing standalone, vaguely hoping it would become my new go-to movie sanctuary. But those aspirations were crushed a few months later when I returned to discover a rubble-strewn lot where the Tippanetr once stood.

That act of destruction became the genesis of this book. If the Tippanetr's loss reflected the state of standalone movie theatres across Thailand, then these buildings needed to be documented while they were still around. In the back of my mind were memories

The Tippanetr Rama theatre, 1990
(courtesy Philippe Doro).

**Opposite:** The auditorium of the Sala Chalerm Krung theatre, Bangkok, circa 1950s.
(courtesy Paisarn Piemmettawat).

11

of the lost movie theatres of my youth in Philadelphia, USA, all of which had been obliterated by the time I reached adulthood. Along with those theatres went a street-side dynamism that has yet to be replicated, even as the city has improved in other ways. Was urban Thailand losing that same variety?

At the time I was pursuing a Masters degree in Sustainable Development at Chiang Mai University, the perfect context for striking out on weekend jaunts to surveil Thailand for old theatres. I set a tentative goal of photographing as many of the remaining theatres as I could before they had their date with the wrecking ball of 'progress'. With Chiang Mai as my base I started to explore the country, travelling between provincial capitals, border towns and remote villages bypassed by time.

The more familiar I became with Thai cinemas, the more I began to identify patterns common to them. Architecturally, Thai movie theatres have a language of their own. Casual observations aside, this fact became ever more clear while visiting with the owner of a dormant theatre in Phichit province who supplemented his anecdotes of the theatre with photos he had carefully preserved in a series of little albums. One album contained a few dozen vintage photos of theatres scattered throughout the nearby provinces. Before he started the process of designing his theatre he had gone on a research trip around the region, surveying theatres already in existence to see what could be achieved architecturally with the

available building materials and construction techniques. The primary aim was to get ideas for a design that would distinguish his theatre from all the rest. It was Thai theatre design influencing Thai theatre design in a closed circuit; a self-perpetuating case of architectural evolution.

By the 1960s, the signature look of a Thai movie theatre featured square facades with bold dimensional signage mounted on the edge of the roof. Sign makers throughout the country crafted some of the most remarkable lettering ever produced to announce the name of each theatre. Set against a typically toned-down architecture, it was these decorative fonts and the neon lighting of the signage that gave Thai movie theatres their strongest identity.

But the most distinct aspects of Thailand's movie theatres were less their physical characteristics than their social function. In the days before most houses had electricity, the local movie theatre was where everybody came together, irrespective of class or occupation. The popularity of Thailand's movie theatres has become a thing of legend today among those old enough to remember. Stories of overflowing crowds spilling into the streets were common. Some witnesses recounted frantic ticket buyers thrusting fists full of cash through the small hole in a ticket window in the hopes of getting into a show before it sold out. In more remote parts of the country, a few theatre owners remembered movie-goers purchasing tickets with links of gold chain broken off from their bracelets or

necklaces, the main form of wealth for rural households. Such was the popularity of movie-going in the days of the standalone.

The pages that follow show photographs of some of Thailand's remaining standalone movie theatres. When I started documenting the theatres in 2008, there were still several dozen standalone theatres in operation across the country, providing a fleeting glimpse of this fading culture as it had endured for much of the previous century. As of this writing, there are no more than three operating nationwide.

Most of the theatres I documented were just shells of their former selves by the time I got to them. Often they were abandoned. Many were complete ruins. For aesthetic reasons, however, those selected for this book tend to be intact, honouring – as much as possible – the look of the theatre from its heyday. Relics of the theatre industry are also on display here: posters, ticket stubs, glass–slide advertisements – scraps of promotional material I was able to collect from the golden age of Thai cinema.

In Thailand, the standalone movie theatre represents a form of public entertainment that has all but slipped through the cracks of memory into the abyss of time. For the last decade and a half, as the trend to demolish old cinemas in Thailand has continued, a full generation of Thais has come of age with little if any knowledge of the outsized role these theatres once played. All the more so for most non-Thais, who, like myself before I started this project, had only experienced a local movie-going culture shackled to shopping malls. To that end, I hope that for Thais and non-Thais alike the images herein will reveal something about Thailand that might otherwise have gone unnoticed.

At the heart of this collection lies a glimmer of hope that the fortunes of the remaining buildings will improve with time. There is currently a fascination among many young Thais for things vintage. Whether this is just the latest aesthetic fad or something more enduring is yet to be seen, but the implications for old movie theatres are interesting. The door to preservation is opening, if only on a crack. For the past two years, Thailand's last movie palace – the legendary Scala theatre (see page 100) – has been in the midst of a slow-motion tug-of-war between a property owner intent on demolishing it and a passionate public that views it as a key piece of Bangkok's modern identity.

But if preservation is not on the cards for Scala and some of Thailand's other historic movie theatres, and if bottom-line business practice trumps all else and not a single standalone survives, I hope that at least some of the romance of escape once found in movie theatre confines will live on in these pages.

Philip Jablon
April 2019

# ROYAL ANTHEM

In Thailand, the Royal Anthem (*Sansoen Phra Barami*) is shown before the start of each film. The audience is required to stand for the duration of the song out of respect for the king. This tradition dates back to the earliest days of cinema in Thailand. In the 1900s, a still image of King Chulalongkorn (Rama V) would be projected onto the screen via a magic lantern slide, while a band played the song. During the reign of the fascist-leaning Field Marshal Plaek Phibulsongkhram, when the monarchy was at its all-time nadir, an image of the prime minister was projected onto movie screens in the same manner. But since the beginning of the reign of King Bhumibol (Rama IX) in 1946, the reigning monarch has been the sole figure screened before films.

# Chapter 1

## EARLY DAYS OF CINEMA: FROM SIAM TO THAILAND

# PRE-WORLD WAR II THEATRES

Motion picture made its debut in Siam (as Thailand was then known) on 10 June 1897 at the Mom Chai Alangkan theatre in Bangkok, approximately two years after the pioneering Lumière brothers premiered the medium in the basement of a Parisian café. Film was an instant success with Siamese audiences, a fact which was not lost on the enterprising eyes of entrepreneurs. As is often the case with new technologies, the medium was first popular among the aristocracy. The first motion picture camera to enter the country was purchased by Prince Thongtham Thavalyavong, a brother of King Chulalongkorn (Rama V), which he used to make his own movies.

The first permanent motion picture theatre, however, was established not by a citizen of Siam, but by a Japanese immigrant who, judging by the success of motion pictures in his native Japan, wisely predicted the popularity they would receive in the Southeast Asian kingdom. In 1905, Watanabe Tomoyori opened the country's first ever movie theatre in Bangkok, calling it "The Japanese Cinema".

From that point onwards, movies and movie theatres proliferated. Dome Sukwong, founder of the Thai Film Archive, estimates that more than 700 theatres were built across Thailand in subsequent years. While the vast majority of those built – and the vast majority of those still in existence – were contracted between the years 1961 and 1981 (see Chapter 2), the years leading up to World War II gave rise to a considerable number.

Many of the earliest movie theatres built in Thailand, specifically in Bangkok, were tucked within the tight confines of *trok* (lane) communities. A fairly common physical configuration in many older Thai urban areas, the *trok* communities consisted of clusters of free-standing wooden houses enclosed by brick-and-mortar shop-houses that lined the streets and canals. Thai communities usually occupied the former while Chinese traders occupied the latter. The interior settlement, where the theatres were built, was accessed through a series of narrow lanes that led from the main thoroughfares and evolved from pathways between the minor canals that interlaced the older areas of the city. These *trok* communities were the culmination of royally-financed road construction, mercantile activity among Chinese businesspeople and a growing number of labourers drawn in from the provinces. The placement of the early movie theatres within *trok* communities was done out of necessity more than anything else; as land on the street-side perimeters of each *trok* was generally occupied by brick shop-houses, the interior courts, interspersed with wooden Thai-style homes, offered sufficient space to build a movie theatre, even if it meant razing some of the houses to make room. For the *trok* communities, these early movie theatres became a dynamic part of the neighbourhood economy and social life. The theatres attracted crowds, who in turn spent money in the *trok*, purchasing snacks and beverages provided by local residents-cum-vendors.

The early movie theatres of Thailand were essentially the living rooms of the communities they served. In a time before most households had electricity, let alone a radio or television, these theatres were their link to the outside world.

In 21st-century Thailand, pre-World War II movie theatres are extremely rare; only a handful still exist nationwide. All of these are currently dormant, except for the Sala Chalerm Krung theatre (also known as the Royal Theatre, see page 26), which is still in use as a live theatre space.

**Previous pages:** Wik Kru Thawee theatre, Ratchaburi province.

**Opposite:** Prince theatre, Bangkok.

# PRINCE THEATRE
## Bang Rak, Bangkok
## 1912-2012

When theatres like the Prince were built, they were the only public venues in which to access cinema. The new communications medium and the theatres that screened it were, in essence, the harbingers of mass society and globalization to come. In a pre-television age, it was the single-screen, standalone cinema hall that was the veritable living room of the community.

The Prince first opened in 1912 as a gambling den catering to the surrounding ethnic Chinese neighbourhood. Following the prohibition of gambling, the building was transformed into a movie theatre in 1917. From then through the 1950s, when the surrounding Bang Rak neighbourhood was a thriving commercial and residential area, the Prince theatre was regarded as one of the premiere theatres in Bangkok. However, by the 1970s it had devolved into a porn theatre and eventually closed in 2012.

The Prince's setting is possibly the most interesting of any movie theatre still standing in Thailand. It is situated behind a wall of shop-houses within a tiny *trok* no more than two metres wide. To modern sensibilities, the Prince's locale seems wholly of another era.

In 2016, the abandoned theatre was acquired by a private developer who has since turned it into a hotel, preserving much of the building and highlighting its former function with film-themed decor, a showcase of items from the original theatre and movie showings in the lobby.

# SALA CHALERM THANI THEATRE

Nang Loeng, Dusit, Bangkok

1918-1993

Nestled in a corner of *trok* Nang Loeng, in the historic Rattanakosin area of Bangkok, stands the Sala Chalerm Thani theatre. More barn in appearance than cinema hall, the mostly wooden structure was contracted by the Siam Cinema Company in 1918 under the name Nang Loeng theatre (by which it is still commonly known today).

In the late 1910s, the Siam Cinema Company became the country's largest theatre operator after two fierce business rivals – the Krungthep Cinematograph Company and the Pathanakorn Film Company – merged into one. The Siam Cinema Company operated as many as 20 movie theatres in and around Bangkok until the early 1930s when financial troubles caused them to sell all their theatres to the newly-formed Siam Niramai Cinema Company, making it the nation's largest theatre chain at the time. It was then that the name of the Nang Loeng theatre was changed to the Sala Chalerm Thani.

By the middle of the century, the theatre was already a relic, eclipsed in comfort and technology by state-of-the-art movie theatres that were sprouting up across the city. In its final years before closing it had become one of the many flophouse porn theatres located throughout Bangkok. Today, new life is being breathed into this old building as its renovation began in 2019 (see Epilogue, page 190).

# SAHA THEATRE
## Songkhla
### 1929-mid-1990s

The ravages of time have been gentle to Songkhla city. The centuries-old seaport has largely been spared the mass reconfigurations of built environments that have done so much to strip the charm out of countless Thai urban areas. Road widening, the demolition of historic buildings and the accompanying paving over of history have only slightly altered the fabric of Songkhla. Indeed, the well-preserved state of Songkhla is a textbook example of how similar old places calcify into what they are. As economic opportunities moved to Songkhla's much larger sister city, Hat Yai, and further afield, so departed much of the town's youthful vitality. Buildings that once housed thriving businesses and workshops were shuttered, while others lingered on thanks to the help of capital accumulated during more prosperous times. The city slowed down, but it didn't die.

Of all the pieces of vintage architecture that make up the streets of Songkhla, there's perhaps none with a more storied past than

the long dormant Saha theatre. Yet, to the average passerby today, the structure would hardly register as a movie theatre. Its lack of architectural elements common to the structural type combined with the fact that it is mostly made of wood (a material not commonly used for movie theatres), places it under the radar of all but the most discerning observers. But to long-time residents, the Saha is a well-known, if not legendary, piece of the town's recent past.

When the Saha theatre opened for business in 1929, originally under the name of Chernchom theatre, the age of the motion picture officially arrived in this bustling port city. Movies became an instant hit, giving rise to a succession of movie theatres in the years to come. With the coming of newer cinemas in the modern era, the Saha became a third-class theatre by Songkhla's standards, eventually closing down for good in the mid-1990s.

The Saha's packed auditorium, circa 1967 (left), the facade in 1971 (opposite), and what remains of the theatre today. (above).

# SALA CHALERM KRUNG THEATRE
## Charoen Krung Road, Bangkok
### 1933-present day

By the late 1920s, cinema had established itself as the entertainment medium of choice among urban Thais, resulting in Bangkok being flush with all kinds of theatres competing for viewership. To honour the city's 150th anniversary in 1932, King Prajadhipok (Rama VII) set aside 300,000 baht from the royal budget for the construction of a modern state-of-the-art theatre with the aim of elevating the theatre industry to world-class standards. The Sala Chalerm Krung theatre was completed in July 1933, one year late of the anniversary. Nonetheless, it set a new standard in movie-theatre design and technology.

In stark departure from the wooden, warehouse-like structures that characterized almost all the early movie theatres in the kingdom, the Sala Chalerm Krung was built of brick and concrete. Its interior was ornately decorated with brass fixtures and comfortable cushioned seats. The major innovation that set it aside from other theatres was the fact that it was air-conditioned, a rarity in an era when electrification was only available in certain quarters.

The Sala Chalerm Krung was a marriage of the most dynamic of the visual arts with the most luxurious of movie theatre design, mostly showcasing Thai cinema for all to enjoy. Even as Bangkok grew and its movie theatre industry evolved, the Sala Chalerm Krung maintained its lofty spot among elite movie theatres in the ever-competitive Bangkok market for decades.

By the early 21st century, however, revenue from film alone was not enough. The multiplex boom siphoned off all but the most dedicated fans and in 2005 the Sala Chalerm Krung Foundation was formed with the goal of finding ways to sustainably maintain the theatre for years to come. The theatre continues to operate to this day, serving as the country's primary venue for masked *khon* classical dance performances and still occasionally screens film.

Clearly visible in this photograph are the tangles of high-tension wires that are synonymous with urban Thailand and feature prominently in almost any street-based photograph.

**Previous page:** Sala Chalerm Krung, 2019 (courtesy Paisarn Piemmettawat).

The Sala Chalerm Krung in its early years, circa 1930s.

The lobby of the Sala Chalerm Krung today, decorated with shadow-play characters from the *Ramakien*, the Thai version of the Ramayana.

**Opposite:** The theatre facade by night shows silhouettes of more *Ramakien* characters, Hanuman (left and right) and the *rishi*, or teacher (centre).

# STATE-BUILT THEATRES

Thailand is politically unique among its neighbours on the Southeast Asian mainland for having avoided a leftist totalitarian regime during the 20th century. Such regimes took ownership of existing theatres or, less frequently, developed new ones from the ground up, all for the purpose of conveying political messages through cinema. Thailand never experienced the outright nationalization of its cinema halls like, say, Burma (today Myanmar) did under the government of General Ne Win, but during the fascistic reign of Field Marshal Plaek Phibulsongkhram, the Thai state was responsible for the development of a handful of theatres.

New Chalerm Uthai theatre, Uthai Thani.

# THAHAN BOK THEATRE
## Lopburi
## 1941-1997

In stark contrast to the vast majority of movie theatres that had opened in other parts of the country by the early 1940s, the Thahan Bok theatre was not built in a typical neighbourhood or market setting. Standing prominently at the far end of the Sa Kaeo traffic circle, the theatre was built as a representation of state planning and efficiency, underscored by what was perceived at the time as the need to create an orderly environment for deployment of military personnel and equipment. The road leading down towards the Sa Kaeo circle from the centre of old Lopburi town is straight and wide, conducive to columns of soldiers marching in a military parade. Situated at the head of this grand causeway, the Thahan Bok theatre served as an expression of both the state's power to protect and to bring the joys of modernity to the population.

In the theatre's early days, military personnel working in and around the nearby Lopburi army base could watch movies for free over the weekend. One of the earliest films to have likely screened here was a propaganda movie produced by Field Marshal Phibulsongkhram himself, entitled *Blood of Thai Soldiers*.

# NEW CHALERM UTHAI THEATRE
## Uthai Thani
### 1943-2001

Like the Thahan Bok theatre in Lopburi (previous page), the New Chalerm Uthai theatre was built by the government of Field Marshal Phibulsongkhram, the nationalist prime minister of Thailand from 1938 to 1944 and 1948 to 1957. Under Phibulsongkhram's administration, Siam was renamed Thailand, the ethnic Chinese community faced severe restrictions on cultural expression, and the adoption of western-style dress and etiquette was encouraged. Many of his policies and political sentiments were made public through propaganda films screened in theatres like this one.

The New Chalerm Uthai theatre, built in 1943, was designed by the same architect as the Thahan Bok theatre and is very similar in style. Both share a sleek Streamline Moderne look common throughout the world during that time, especially among government building projects. Since the New Chalerm Uthai was built on land once occupied by a temple, the land and the theatre itself are owned by the government Religious Affairs Department.

It closed down in 2001, though in recent years there has been some talk of having it turned into a local museum.

# Chapter 2

## THE BOOM YEARS:
## 1961-1981

Starting around 1961, the construction of modernist standalone movie theatres, built primarily of brick and concrete (as opposed to wood), began in haste throughout Thailand. Their proliferation helped usher Thailand into the era of mass-market consumerism and industrialization.

The year 1961 was important for Thailand for another reason: it was the year the governments of Thailand and the United States entered into a strategic partnership with the two-pronged aim of bolstering Thailand against communism, which had been gaining momentum across the region, and pushing back against communist forces in neighbouring countries. Central to this partnership was Thailand's permission for the US Air Force to station aircraft at six Royal Thai Airforce bases, from where America would fly reconnaissance and bombing missions against targets in Laos and Vietnam.

Many millions of dollars were poured into the Thai economy over the ensuing years, some of which were earmarked specifically for economic development programmes. Other money came through military spending, as R&R economies developed in towns hosting US military personnel. The influx of dollars stimulated wide-reaching social change, spurring infrastructure development and market integration in even the most far-flung corners of the country. With growing wealth and disposable incomes, a taste for cinema blossomed and, for the next 20 years or so, standalone movie theatres were constructed in nearly every district in every province of the country.

In provincial towns nationwide, theatre owners were usually drawn from local business families of ethnic Chinese descent who had accumulated capital from years of dealing in various agricultural goods and services. As rural markets expanded, these countryside capitalists built movie theatres on land often located at or near rural trading centres. By the 1970s, a striking new movie theatre was a common feature of small towns across the Thai hinterland.

The theatre boom provided international movie distributors with a healthy market in Thailand. Although dominated by imports from Hollywood, the international viewing fare included films from Hong Kong, Japan, India and Europe. Due to this diversity, the movie theatre became a wellspring of globalization for the average person in Thailand. Moreover, at no other period in Thai history was there a more international assortment of films screening in Thai theatres at any given time.

The domestic film industry also flourished, breaking with tradition in order to keep stride with technical innovations from abroad. An increase in the number and quality of films minted a fresh batch of superstars, as names like Mitr Chaibancha, Petchara Chaowarat, Lor Dok and Sombath Methanee – to name just a few – rose to prominence. But the biggest change came as 35 mm film began to replace 16 mm as the format of choice. Aside from the larger, more robust picture made possible by 35 mm, it also made it possible to record sound onto the film. During the 16 mm era, due to the lack of soundtrack on the film stock, a typical Thai film relied on live voice actors (see The Dubbers, page 172) to speak the parts of the on-screen cast and narrators. With 35 mm, live dubbers became unnecessary, forever changing the way Thai films were made and consumed. Bigger, more technologically advanced theatres were built to accommodate the increasingly sophisticated movies being made.

As the 1980s rolled in, however, the theatre construction boom began to slow down. Changing technology and the rise of home entertainment diminished the need for massive, single-screen theatres. Ticket sales declined accordingly and theatres slowly began to close.

In the 1990s, several theatre chains struck deals with shopping mall developers to include multiplex theatres on the top floors. The multiplex turned out to be a disruptive technology, cutting ever deeper into the market share of the older standalone variety. Additionally, the proliferation of home entertainment systems – TVs, VCRs and karaoke machines – combined with an increase in car ownership, made trips to local standalone movie theatres (which often did not provide parking) less appealing, if not altogether inconvenient.

By the 2000s, shopping malls were all the rage in Thai urban centres, able to attract the car-driving consumer base with secure parking garages on location. Once inside, the added options of shopping and eating as well as seeing a movie at the multiplex theatre, all under one climate-controlled roof, pushed standalone theatres into the margins of consumer society. In short, the rise of the shopping mall marked the death of the standalone movie theatre in Thailand.

**Previous pages:** Charoen Rath theatre, Khon Kaen (courtesy Philippe Doro).　　　**Opposite:** Petch Siam theatre, Sukhothai province.

# SRI NAKHON THEATRE
## Hang Chat, Lampang province
### 1957-1970

The Sri Nakhon theatre faces onto Hang Chat's main thoroughfare, diverging architecturally from the avenue's other structures by little more than the free-standing signage perched on the edge of its roof. The inventory of buildings is composed of a discernibly older stock than most small towns in the Thai north and the main street's visual uniformity has a soothing aspect to it, reflecting the aesthetic conservatism of mid-20th century provincial Thailand.

For all intents and purposes, Hang Chat is a suburb of the much larger and economically dynamic provincial capital, Lampang. Travel between the two has been simple and unobstructed since they were connected by railway in the early 1920s. As a result, the Sri Nakhon was never able to attract large crowds because by the time a film made its way there, all the townsfolk and people from the surrounding villages had already seen it at one of the bigger theatres in Lampang. The theatre quietly closed down in 1970 and has been empty ever since.

# PHAYAO RAMA THEATRE
## Phayao
## 1958-2010

Modern multiplexes in Thailand are seldom ever built in the middle of town. Those that are, such as a few in Bangkok and one in Chiang Mai, are situated atop shopping malls and generally designed so that viewers can drive into a parking garage to get there. In other words, the movie-goer doesn't have to engage with the city streets on foot when going to watch a movie. At the Phayao Rama on the other hand, after watching the beautifully shot gore fest *Meat* *Grinder* in 2009, I left the theatre and was immediately deposited in the centre of a deserted city. The walk back to my hotel, past shuttered shops and restaurants lining the empty streets of Phayao, gave me the opportunity to digest what I had just seen, unburdened by the responsibilities of driving; that solitary stroll, amplified by the lingering effects of cinema, was both exhilarating and sobering at the same time.

# WATHANA THEATRE
## Takhli, Nakhon Sawan province
## 1961-1970

The United States Air Force began building and using military facilities in Thailand as early as 1961, mostly as a precaution against the 'falling dominoes' theory, which purported that if Vietnam, Laos and Cambodia were to become communist states, Thailand would be next and the US would lose another client. By 1965, the US was fully engaged in the Vietnam War and six Thai airports were hosting American military aircraft and personnel. The base at Takhli played host to a number of fighting squadrons flying missions over Laos and Vietnam. As a result of the American military presence, Takhli was awash with dollars. In 1961, the Wathana theatre became the first of four movie theatres to dot the landscape of the little city.

The Wathana is a good example of a theatre built on the cusp of Thailand's movie theatre boom. In terms of design it was more closely related to the stock of theatres being built before World War II than those constructed mid century. Ceiling fans were the only way to cool patrons, whereas most theatres built later were equipped with air-conditioning. The theatre also had balcony seating, generally an older architectural form than stadium seating.

# MA WIN RAMA THEATRE
## Ban Rai, Sukhothai province
### 1972-1994

The village of Ban Rai is situated about seven kilometres outside Sukhothai city and, like many villages in the lower north of Thailand, owes its existence to its past as a trading hub for agricultural goods. The local market drew farmers and farmhands from the surrounding fields. A town, in all its bucolic modesty, sprang up around it.

In the middle decades of the 20th century, the jungles of upper Thailand were being felled to make way for the expansion of market-based agriculture. Local business entrepreneurs who dealt in agricultural products and services tended to prosper from the increased production, which became known the world over as the Green Revolution. In 1972, the owner of Ban Rai's main market, having profited handsomely from Green Revolution expansion, decided to diversify his business holdings. With a high volume of foot traffic already in place, he surmised that building a movie theatre on the grounds of his market would be a natural fit; similar marketplace and movie-theatre combinations were being developed across Thailand in response to the country's increased appetite for film.

Home electrification in rural Thailand was not yet widespread in the early 1970s and if villagers living in the vicinity of Ban Rai wanted a dose of modern entertainment they had to travel all the way to Sukhothai city for a movie theatre. Opening a theatre in Ban Rai thus made practical sense.

Enter the Ma Win Rama. For the first 20 years of its existence, the Ma Win Rama was predictably successful. To nearby villagers, it was the most immediate entertainment venue – one of the only local spaces to offer a window onto another world, or a fictitious reflection of their own. But, as houses were wired for electricity and different mediums for viewing movies became more widespread, the Ma Win Rama began to lose customers, if not its standing as an important community gathering point. In the mid-1990s, the theatre was closed. The owner went on to invest in a tour-bus company, which connects Sukhothai with points near and far, and contains an echo of the defunct theatre in its name – Win Tour.

# KHEMSAWAT THEATRE
## Fang, Chiang Mai province
### 1975-2004

The Khemsawat was the first theatre in Fang built of brick and mortar. Declining attendance led to its closure before it reached its 30th anniversary. It is noteworthy for the use of terracotta tiles on the facade, an uncommon aesthetic feature among Thai movie theatres.

# AMARIN RAMA THEATRE
## Sawankhalok, Sukhothai province
### 1976-1992

The Amarin Rama once stood in a commercial plaza anchored by the theatre. The shops and restaurants in the plaza catered to the hundreds of daily patrons who spent their free time watching movies there. Business owners in the plaza made a nice living but when the Amarin Rama was put out of business in 1992 by home theatres and other technological innovations, the entire plaza died with it.

Like most of the other standalone movie theatres in Thailand, the Amarin Rama was once the most popular place in town. A resident of the plaza, Att, recalled that the theatre was packed every day in the 1970s and '80s. On public holidays, the theatre would hold extra showings to accommodate the larger crowds. "Now there's no place in town to see a movie," lamented Att. "Sawankhalok used to have a second theatre, too, but it's been torn down." In 2011, the Amarin Rama was also demolished.

มาเป็นกองทัพ ฟ้าสะท้าน ดินสะเทือน โลกร้าว

# คอนวอย

280 ล้าน
**EMI** "แซม เพ็คคินพ่าห์"
สร้างประวัติศาสตร์หนัง

คริส คริส
อาลี แมคคา
เออร์เนส

ฉายที่         วันที่

# CHALERM POR THEATRE
## Pak Chong, Nakhon Ratchasima province
### 1957-2011

The Chalerm Por theatre was built in 1957, the same year that the Mittraphap Highway linking Isan with central Thailand opened. Originally it was a theatre for *likay* (Thai musical drama) but switched over to showing film by the early 1960s. These images were taken in 2010, a year before it closed, when it was the oldest movie theatre still operating in Thailand. The foyer is depicted overleaf.

# VISTA THEATRE
## Udon Thani
### 1967-1998

The Vista theatre was contracted in 1967 by a doctor-turned-businessman known throughout town as *Mor* (doctor) Sukhum. Having achieved great success and local celebrity with the establishment of Udon Thani's first private hospital, *Mor* Sukhum expanded into the movie exhibition business. Demand for film at the time was heightened by American airmen stationed at the nearby Wing 23 Airbase. In the 1960s and early 1970s, Udon Thani was a boom town with a war-time economy linked to the Vietnam War that resulted in the development of much of the city as it stands today. The flourishing economy spawned ever-larger movie theatres as the influx of cash created greater disposable incomes for spending on leisure activities.

This golden age for theatres like the Vista, however, was short-lived. Technological changes and macro-level demographic shifts made 1,200-seat theatres unnecessarily large and difficult to maintain. After just over 30 years of operation, the Vista screened its last film – John Woo's action-thriller *Face/Off* – on 11 May 1998.

# THEPBANTERNG THEATRE
## Nong Khai
### 1971-1997

The Thepbanterng theatre was built by Yiamjit Thepbanterng and her husband in 1971. At the time, Nong Khai was playing a strategic role in the American effort to undermine communist forces in neighbouring Laos; the capital of Laos, Vientiane, is just across the river from Nong Khai. Yiamjit recalls renting out the entire top floor of her family's Thepbanterng hotel to CIA agents. The hotel was situated in front of the theatre and she said American military personnel spent a portion of their down-time in the Thepbanterng theatre's soundtrack room (pictured above, see page 69 for more detail on soundtrack rooms at the Burapha theatre).

The Thepbanterng closed its doors for good during the 1997 Asian financial crisis.

# AMARIN THEATRE

## Loei

### 1978-2012

The Amarin theatre was Loei's blue-hued dream factory. For upwards of two decades it was the town's cultural aorta, a cinematic ventricle and beacon of something to do in an otherwise quiet little town.

In 2010, ten minutes before the 8pm start of *Confucius*, starring Chow Yun-fat, the owner of the Amarin theatre, Phanida, was still holding out hope that at least a few of the Loei faithful would have the time and interest to take in a movie. "Business is not good," she admitted, seated behind the ticket window. "Every now and then we have a decent day, but not when a Chinese movie is showing. Chinese productions don't really have the same drawing power that they used to."

I waited and waited, hoping to document a theatre lobby abuzz with action, but it was a slow night at the Amarin. Including myself, the turn-out was less than a dozen. Phanida and the other theatre staff were warm and accommodating nonetheless, welcoming a photo session and happy to talk about movies and the theatre business in general. Dating only to 1978, the Amarin was the second movie theatre venture undertaken by Phanida's family; an elder sibling built the now-closed Petch Rama back in the late 1960s. When questioned about the Amarin's future in the face of paltry ticket sales, Phanida smiled, playfully raising a fist and exclaiming, "We're fighting on!"

In 2012, two years after that poorly-attended showing of *Confucius*, the Amarin closed.

# SOMDET THEATRE
## Somdet, Kalasin province
### 1981-1991

Somdet, the town after which this theatre is named, seems an odd location for a theatre of such mass. But in the theatre's inaugural year of 1981, Somdet and its surrounding villages had yet to be linked to the electricity grid. Powered by means of a diesel generator, the Somdet theatre was the premier destination for nearby farmers and townsfolk alike. Being the only such venue between Kalasin and Mukdahan, it had to account for the entertainment of lots of people, thus warranting its cavernous size and title as the province's largest theatre.

By the mid-1980s, electrification had been duly applied to Somdet district and movie-goers, normally dependent on the cinema for their entertainment needs, began to opt for domestic television and its accoutrements instead. Profits dwindled as attendance shrank and, just ten years after its inception, the Somdet went out of business.

นักรบ
เดนตาย

มันบาดเป็นกองทัพ
แต่ข้าจะยืมอยู่คนเดียว
เพื่อศักดิ์ศรีของความเป็นคน

ซิลเวสเตอร์
สตอลโลน

**FIRST BLOOD**

MARIO KASSAR and ANDREW VAJNA Present

A TED KOTCHEFF Film

SYLVESTER STALLONE  FIRST BLOOD  RICHARD CRENNA

Starring BRIAN DENNEHY Music by JERRY GOLDSMITH Director of Photography ANDREW LASZLO Executive Producers MARIO KASSAR and ANDREW VAJNA
Co-Executive Producer HERB NANAS Produced by BUZZ FEITSHANS Screenplay by MICHAEL KOZOLL & WILLIAM SACKHEIM and SYLVESTER STALLONE
Based on the novel by DAVID MORRELL Directed by TED KOTCHEFF  An ORION PICTURES Release

ดังดับโลก

ซิลเวสเตอร์ สตอลโลน
ความมันส์ทั้งโลกมารวมอยู่ในคนๆเดียว

ริชาร์ด เครนน่า / สต

CAROLCO  TRI STAR PICTURES

MARIO KASSAR and ANDREW VAJNA present SYLVESTER STALLONE "RAMBO / FIRST BLOOD PART
Screenplay by SYLVESTER STALLONE and JAMES CAMERON  Story by KEVIN JARRE  Based on characters created by

# COLD WAR RURAL DEVELOPMENT AND THE RISE OF THE CINEMA HALL

In the 1960s and '70s, while the Vietnam War was raging to the east of Thailand and a communist movement was growing domestically, the difficult-to-access wilds of rural Nan province became a safe haven for both Thai and Lao communists. The area's historical disconnection from the rest of the country and proximity to Laos made the Bangkok political establishment wary of the potential for Nan to develop into a communist training ground. As the Vietnam War came to a close in 1975, with newly established communist governments sweeping to power in Laos, Cambodia and Vietnam, refugees fled across the porous Thai-Lao border with many coming into Nan province. They were seen by the Thai government as a further threat to national security.

Fear of an insurgency in Nan spurred the activation of road construction projects into the hinterlands during the 1970s. It was believed that bringing the largely rural population of Nan under the veil of the modern, national economy would prevent insurgents – both homegrown and foreign – from building a support base there.

Engineering firms from far and wide were awarded contracts to build roads and other infrastructure projects. In 1976, a young civil engineer named Pornsak Anugkawanit was hired by the Italian-Thai Company to help in a road-construction project designed to link some of the more remote districts of Nan to the national road network. Pornsak, a native of Phuket province, had spent very little time in the north but, as he settled in for a prolonged period of work in the Pua district of Nan, he quickly adjusted to northern culture. Pornsak met a local girl named Surang, the daughter of Chinese-born merchant parents and operators of an old wooden movie theatre. Soon thereafter, Pornsak and Surang were married, settling down in Pua town for the duration of the road-construction project. When the project was complete and Pornsak's contract with the Italian-Thai Company had been fulfilled, the couple turned their attention to the movie theatre run by Surang's family. The young couple predicted that the completed road system would enable agricultural products from the surrounding countryside to quickly reach the national market and beyond, bringing prosperity to the area. With that in mind, in 1979, they invested the savings

Pornsak had amassed while working for the Italian-Thai Company in the construction of a brick-and-cement movie theatre near the centre of the town, just a few hundred metres from the road Pornsak had helped engineer. They named the theatre after the town it stood in and the Pua Rama was born.

Most of Pua, and indeed the rest of rural Thailand, did not yet have access to private televisions and movie theatres were one of the few places people could go to for modern entertainment. As such, Pornsak and Surang created one of the most popular venues in town. Throughout most of the 1980s their theatre was hugely successful. Each night it was packed with people who came to watch movies from as far away as remote Bo Klua district. Residents of the town and nearby villages made the Pua Rama their go-to place for entertainment. On weekends and national holidays, the turn-out was so high that the theatre sold standing-room only tickets.

By the early 1990s, however, just a little over ten years after it opened, Pornsak and Surang saw sharp declines in theatre attendance. Household electrification and the accompanying growth of home entertainment technology had become available in Pua and what was once a night at the movies for a typical family turned into a night at home in front of the TV. Despite lagging ticket sales, they held on through most of the 1990s. They lowered ticket prices and began running double features to attract customers but nothing seemed to work. The population of small towns like Pua was diminishing; an unintended consequence of the stronger market integration made possible by the construction of the road networks.

In 1997, the Asian financial crisis struck Thailand. Many banks across the country saw major defaults on loan payments, leaving them cash strapped and unable to dispense further loans. This caused a ripple effect across the country and small businesses suffered, the Pua Rama among them. Pornsak and Surang held on for another two years before showing their last movie at the Pua Rama in 1999.

The Pua Rama theatre in Pua, Nan province, was built in 1979 and closed in 1999.

# DARA THEATRE
## Trat
### mid-1970s-early 2000s

There's something about the Dara theatre as it stands today – weathered, soot-stained and forgotten – that places it, not only from another time period, but from another world altogether. Today, with people so absorbed in consumerism, distracted by smart phones and gadgetry and beholden to the car or motorbike for movement, it's hard to imagine they would ever have had time to waste on such a building. The reality is that the Dara was indeed short lived – just a blip in Thai history that left behind an interesting piece of architecture.

# BURAPHA THEATRE
## Ban Chang, Rayong province
### 1974-1997

The Burapha theatre was brought into existence by Sompong Chotiwan who, by 1974, was already an established figure in the movie exhibition industry of Bangkok and eastern Thailand. Based out of the much older Nang Loeng theatre (see page 22) in Bangkok, both his birthplace and the nerve centre of Thailand's film industry, also made him well situated to be a movie distributor. His company, Mueang Chol Films, was the biggest distributor of films in eastern Thailand.

Then, as today, movie distributors divided Thailand into regional zones where only select companies could operate. Each distribution company purchased the rights to a film from the various production houses, usually headquartered in Bangkok, and then circulated it to theatres within their respective networks. Some distributors built their own theatres or purchased pre-existing theatres within their network, thus eliminating the need to share profits with independent theatre owners; a fairly common practice that became a fast track to empire for successful film exhibitors.

By the early 1970s, the town of Ban Chang had benefited economically from its proximity to the U-Tapao Airbase, one of six airbases in Thailand hosting the United States Air Force during the Vietnam War. With the town awash in money thanks to a base full of foreign soldiers, cutting-edge leisure facilities became a necessity. The town already boasted two active theatres, one of which, the Ban Chang Rama, was also owned and operated by Sompong. But the resident English-speaking population at the nearby airbase were at a linguistic deficit when it came to watching movies, even when the movies themselves were American made.

Until the mid-1980s, most Thai theatres employed live voice actors to give foreign movies a Thai voice track. Original in-film soundtracks were muted while dubbers read from a Thai script written to fit the plot. Sometimes story lines were modified to suit Thai tastes and dialogue was improvised on the spot (see *Serpico*, page 173). For the Thai public, a good dubber was an essential part of the movie-going experience. For non-Thai speakers, however, it made the films inaccessible. Necessity being what it is to invention, Thai theatre entrepreneurs accommodated their English-speaking clientele by building 'soundtrack rooms' – small, air-conditioned seating sections behind a large glass window into which a speaker system separate from the main auditorium played the original language soundtrack so that spectators therein could watch the film along with the rest of the audience (see image on page 57). Down below, the Thai dubbers worked their magic and everyone was happy.

**Overleaf:** The interior of the Burapha, much diminished from its heyday.

# CHANTHABURI MULTIPLEX
## Chanthaburi
### 1980-2011

The theatre opened in 1980 as the Chanthaburi Rama, an 880-seat single screener that replaced a decrepit wooden theatre called the Sin Tu Nawa, which had occupied the same plot of land for decades.

By the late 1980s, four newer theatres had been constructed across Chanthaburi, giving the town one of the densest concentrations of standalone movie theatres anywhere in Thailand. While this scenario must have been great for film enthusiasts, it made for stiff competition among theatre owners. As an adaptive measure, the owners of the Chanthaburi Rama divided their grand cinema hall into four smaller theatres in the mid-1990s to create one of Thailand's first multiplex theatres. The procedure turned out to be a wise one; with four potential viewing options, the Chanthaburi Multiplex (as it was renamed) could offer the same viewing fare as all the other movie theatres in town combined.

One by one, Chanthaburi's other theatres closed their doors, while the Chanthaburi Multiplex hung on until a brand new SF Cinema (Thailand's second largest cinema operator) opened a branch in a new shopping mall just outside of the downtown area in 2011.

# SIRI PHANOM RAMA THEATRE

## Phanom Sarakham,
## Chachoengsao province

### 1978-2014

Located on the far edge of the little trading town of Phanom Sarakham, the Siri Phanom Rama is one of the most definitively Brutalist cinema halls ever seen in the country. Completed in 1978 as the economic anchor of a surrounding retail-and-residential complex built simultaneously, the Siri Phanom Rama was the third theatre erected in the district and will probably be the last. The small sign to the left of the entrance notes that the building is closed for renovation but it is unlikely to open again as a movie theatre.

# SA KAEO RAMA THEATRE
## Sa Kaeo
### 1983-1997

From a few choice vantage points the Sa Kaeo Rama calls to mind a ruin from a lost civilization left abandoned to the jungle's verdant stranglehold. While the ruinous aspect holds true at ground level, the reality is that the abandoned theatre stands amid a failed development on the edge of the city, not an encroaching jungle. It was a product of urban expansion on the heels of a highway extension and the-sky's-the-limit confidence brought on by automobile accessibility. Thailand has no shortage of these kinds of blighted peri-urban cityscapes; they line the edges of arterial roads like phantom reminders of failed civilizations. This particular iteration originally housed a fresh market and the local bus station along with the cinema hall. Whatever order the collapse occurred in is unclear but a mostly vacant business centre is the sad result.

Had the Sa Kaeo Rama been contracted in the years before developers enthusiastically supported projects that followed the highway, it might have been erected in the centre of old Sa Kaeo, accessible by foot to a pedestrian-oriented population. The theatre's architecture and scale are conducive to middle-of-the-block placement in a high-density zone and one can imagine both its bold signage and textured modernist facade serving as a visual (and social) anchor to the traditional core of Sa Kaeo.

Even in its present run-down condition the Sa Kaeo Rama is a sight to behold. Being removed from a practical location, conveniently accessed by motor transport alone, ensures that it remains a hidden spot to all except locals and any visitor so inquisitive as to ask, "Excuse me, but does your town have any old movie theatres?"

# MUEANG THONG RAMA THEATRE
## Singburi
### 1969-2000

The Mueang Thong Rama opened in 1969 as the Khu Rak (couples) theatre. Some time in the 1970s the name was changed to Mueang Thong Rama. With its modernist lancet arches supporting an open-air pavilion lobby and grand floating staircase, the Mueang Thong Rama is one of the more unique theatres in Thailand and sits on the banks of the Chao Phraya river in what used to be the centre of Singburi's port district.

# MAHACHAI RAMA THEATRE
## Mahachai, Samut Sakhon province
## 1972-2012

It must have been an amazing sight to look down Soi Baan Chao towards the Mahachai Rama thirty or forty years ago. Back then, the bold dimensional signage would have been accentuated by neon lighting with giant hand-painted movie billboards fastened to the theatre's facade. It was the visual pinnacle of Mahachai. Even in its current rundown condition, the Mahachai Rama remains the single most enticing vista in town.

# FAH SIAM THEATRE
## Suphanburi
## 1972-2012

Few works of Thai theatre architecture have generated the same amount of interest as the Fah Siam theatre has since I began documenting Thai movie theatres in 2008. Like many of the structures built in Suphanburi during the middle decades of the 20th century, the Fah Siam was contracted by the province's now-deceased political godfather, Banharn Silpa-Archa. It was the anchor business of Loet Fah market, where food and dry goods vendors set up shop in its shadow for many a year.

The demolition of the Fah Siam theatre in 2013, a year after it closed, epitomizes the fate of this structural type throughout Thailand despite its singularly unique architecture. Once the Fah Siam had outlived its initial role as a movie theatre, the building was demolished in favour of a more lucrative apartment house, which carries none of the architectural or cultural merit of the theatre it replaced. So long as a nationwide inertia towards architectural heritage remains, more stunning buildings – theatres or otherwise – will continue to be lost, even when the potential for revival looms on the horizon.

When these photographs were taken the Fah Siam was under the ownership of the Thana Cineplex, hence the alternative name in the entranceway.

# BANG PA-IN RAMA THEATRE
## Bang Pa-In, Ayutthaya province
### 1981-1996

When the province of Ayutthaya developed into one of Thailand's primary industrial hubs in the early 1980s, the demand for transportation by labourers going to-and-from factories increased. In response, a family by the name of Jiamboonseth, having relocated from Chachoengsao province, developed the Bang Pa-In Commerce Centre as a mixed-use development containing retail shops and a bus depot with the Bang Pa-In Rama at its nucleus.

The placement of cinema halls in proximity to transit hubs was common practice in years past and was one of the more typical couplings of 20th-century modern infrastructure. Movie theatres often sprang up near train stations but bus depots also had theatres in close proximity. The reason was simple: passengers arriving from far and wide at a given transit station often have time to kill, and movies are one of the great passtimes.

At the Bang Pa-In Rama, movie-goers had to ascend to the third floor to reach the auditorium of this late-era International Style theatre. The upper lobby is now occupied by a billiards hall.

# KAMPHAENG SAEN RAMA THEATRE
## Kamphaeng Saen, Nakhon Pathom province
### 1982-1999

The Kamphaeng Saen Rama was the second movie theatre to open in Kamphaeng Saen and was the more luxurious of the two, giving it an immediate advantage over its older competitor, the Trisuk theatre, which was tucked away in the town's central market. With the opening of the Kamphaeng Saen Rama, the town's movie-going market became over-saturated, leading to a decline in ticket sales at the Trisuk, which closed down soon thereafter.

Aside from advantages in comfort and technology, differences in location also played a critical role in the Kamphaeng Saen Rama's survival over the Trisuk. In the early 1980s, Thailand's industrial boom was just beginning to take off and the wealth created led to a further proliferation of car ownership, especially in the central provinces where most of the industry was situated. New car owners, pining to show off their new wheels, would have found parking difficult in the close quarters of the central market where the older Trisuk theatre stood. The Kamphaeng Saen Rama, on the other hand, was built on the outskirts of town, along the highway leading towards the provincial capital. Parking was abundant in the surrounding fields, thus making a trip to the pictures less of a hassle. By the turn of the 21st century, however, the Kamphaeng Saen Rama was also out of business.

# SIAM THEATRE
## Siam Square, Bangkok
### 1966-2010

The Siam theatre was the original flagship theatre of the Pyramid Company (the original name of the Apex Company). It opened on 15 December 1966 with the Thai premiere of *Battle of the Bulge* starring Henry Fonda. The theatre was slated to be named the Chula theatre in honour of King Chulalongkorn (Rama V) but on the advice of Kukrit Pramoj, a leading statesmen and later Prime Minister of Thailand, the name was shelved in favour of Siam. The surrounding neighbourhood was soon dubbed Siam Square after the theatre that spearheaded its development.

The Siam was groundbreaking on multiple fronts. It was the first Thai movie theatre equipped with the Cinerama projection system, elevating the movie-watching experience to new levels for Thai audiences. Hundreds of Thai theatres built subsequently would use the abbreviated 'rama' of Cinerama fame in their names to denote a cutting-edge place to watch a film (e.g. Bangkok Rama, Hat Yai Rama or Sakkarin Rama), despite the fact that the technology was more often absent than present.

Like Cinerama, escalators, too, made their Thai premiere at the Siam theatre when a pair was installed in the open-air bi-level lobby to effortlessly transport patrons to the grand 800-seat auditorium.

By the 1980s, the Siam had developed a reputation as one of Bangkok's main theatres for art-house and independent movies. Foreign films were screened with their original language soundtracks, preserving the cadence of each film for the satisfaction of Bangkok's most dedicated cinephiles. Like its sister theatres, the Lido and the Scala, the Siam experienced a drastic downturn in attendance as the number of multiplex theatres increased across the capital. On 19 May 2010, the Siam was set on fire amid a violent crackdown by the Thai military on anti-government protesters. It burned beyond the point of salvation and was later completely demolished.

*Battle of the Bulge* was the first movie screened at the Siam theatre on the night it opened, 15 December 1966.

ในระบบไดเมนชั่น 150
# D-150
ฟิล์ม 70 มม. จอโค้ง 120 องศา
ระบบเสียงแม็คเนติก 6 แถบเสียง
ลำโพง 17 ตัวรอบโรง

ครีเอชั่น
CREATION

BATTLE OF THE BULGE
ฉวไฟว์สตาร์ จัดจำหน่าย
โท. 2811558·2811800

ดาราดังมาพบกัน
มากว่า 50 คน.

เฮนรี่ ฟอนดา
ชาร์ลส์ บรอนสัน
โรเบิร์ต ชอว์
โรเบิร์ต ไรอัน
เทลลี่ ซาวาลาส
บาบารา เวิร์ล
ดานา แอนดรูส์
เจมส์ แม็คอาเธอร์
เปียร์ แองเจลี
ฯลฯ

วันที่                                        นี้

# LIDO THEATRE
## Siam Square, Bangkok
### 1968-2018

When the Lido Theatre first opened its doors on 27 June 1968, the Siam Square neighbourhood it stands in saw its inventory of sleek, modern movie palaces double overnight. The Siam theatre, which stood about 100 metres away, had been built two years earlier and initiated the neighbourhood's transformation from a peri-urban slum to Bangkok's main commercial hub. With the Lido, the area coalesced into one of Bangkok's most vital shopping and entertainment zones. Through the 1970s and '80s, the Lido was considered one of Bangkok's premiere movie theatres, steadily providing a first-class cinema experience.

In 1992, fire struck the Lido, completely destroying its grand auditorium. Instead of using the tragedy as a pretext to divest itself of the aging theatre, Apex – the parent company of the Lido, Siam

**Above:** The facade of the Lido in the year it opened, 1968.
**Opposite:** The Lido not long before it closed down, obscured by the Siam Square station of the Bangkok Sky Train.

and Scala – reopened it a year or so later as a three-screen multiplex. The modification was a prescient one. Within less than a decade Rama I Road would be lined with shopping malls, each consisting of a multiplex theatre. Dividing the Lido into three screens made competing with the new multiplexes viable. In addition to the architectural modifications, programming was also updated and, following on from the Siam, the Lido became Bangkok's go-to theatre for art-house and foreign films, endearing itself to the city's small but passionate community of cinephiles.

By the dawn of the new century, Bangkok was fast becoming a crowded movie-theatre market. While most of the city's stock of ageing standalone theatres was on the wane, a new generation of multiplex theatres was cropping up in shopping malls across the city. With them came the all-in-one convenience of shopping, eating, free parking and multiple films to choose from all under one high-tech, low-brow, climate-controlled roof. Malls caught on like wild fire among Bangkokians and became the new symbolic standard for middle-class consumerism. Meanwhile, the Lido and its Siam Square siblings – the Siam and the Scala – held tight, ramping up their specialized viewing fare as a means of staying relevant. But, at the end of 2017, the Apex Company announced it would not be renewing its lease on the Lido. It screened its last film – the Japanese romance *Tonight, at the Movies* – on 31 May 2018, less than one month short of its 50th birthday.

# SCALA THEATRE
## Siam Square, Bangkok
### 1969-present day

The Scala is Bangkok's last movie palace – a lone survivor from an era in Thai history when standalone cinema halls were built to world-class standards. The 1960s through the late '70s marked the peak of their nationwide accession, as hundreds of buildings were contracted to fill a growing demand for cinema.

Arguably the most elegant of all the theatres built during that boom, the Scala holds a part-sentimental, part awe-inspiring place in the hearts and minds of Thailand's movie lovers. Its architecture alone – a uniquely Thai composite of tropical art deco and 1960s Thai modern – is a good reason to visit. The simple act of entering its sumptuous open-air lobby is an effective remedy for anybody seeking a break from Bangkok's grinding street-life; pedestrians pop in regularly for that sole purpose. The Scala has a vaulted lobby ceiling, upheld by concrete pillars that resemble alabaster stalactites. Each overhead depression contains a gold-coloured medallion, star-shaped and luminescent with its lone, dimly-lit bulb.

At the landing of the imperial staircase, joining the lower and upper lobbies, hangs a five-tiered chandelier comprised of hundreds of frosted glass spheres. This fixture lends itself glowingly to cinematic glamour and would mark the zenith of decor in the Scala were it not surpassed in artistry by the 50-foot long plaster wall relief above the auditorium entrance. Designed by Filipino artist Ver V. Manipol, the linear work is called Asia Holiday and depicts entwining vignettes of Asian civilizations in an overwrought mid-century style.

The list of aesthetic delights could go on and on without mention of the Scala's movie theatre function, which, after all, is its most endearing aspect. When the Scala opened for business in 1969, 70 mm film was in trend – similar to IMAX today. At double the size of standard 35 mm film, 70 mm could be projected larger and crisper, enhancing the movie-watching experience. Huge concave screens suitable for handling this jumbo format were required for the full effect to be realized and the Scala was built with this technology in place.

While most of the old theatres designed for 70 mm are now gone, the Scala stands as a rare holdover. Its 70 mm system is no longer in use but the screen is still immense, as is the auditorium itself, with its ocean of 800 seats arranged upon a gently sloping gradient. There's not a bad angle in the entire house, further underscoring the Scala as a staple among connoisseurs of film.

The Scala's fate rests in the hands of the Property Management Office of Chulalongkorn University, landlord of the theatre and surrounding Siam Square neighbourhood. In 2012, the university announced plans that called for the demolition of the Scala, its less-ornate sister theatre, Lido, and the surrounding three-story shop-house community that comprises the Siam Square neighbourhood. The cleared land would be used to build a series of shopping malls, aimed at driving up revenue for the university. Immediately following the announcement, a chorus of opposition erupted across Thai media, citing Scala's unique architectural merits and its distinction as one of the last operating standalone movie theatres in a city once packed with them. Sustained public pressure combined with less-than-ideal economic circumstances led officials at the university to respond with a series of lease extensions to the Apex Company, which runs the theatres. As of this writing, there is a movement from within the university to come up with a viable plan for maintaining the Scala as a working movie theatre.

# THE YELLOW JACKETS

The Scala is full of elements that easily sear into one's memory. Most of them are to do with the lavish architecture, such as the modernist imperial staircase that conveys movie-goers from atrium to lobby in high style, passing beneath the five-tiered frosted glass chandelier. More design splendour awaits on the second level. But it's not an architectural element that is the most endearing part of this landmark cinema; that compliment goes to the famed 'Yellow Jackets', the pineapple-hued ushers who let in one and all.

Since the company's founding in 1949, the Apex chain – parent company of the Scala – has been dressing its ushers and ticket takers in bright yellow blazers. The signature attire, donned with understated pride by those who tear tickets and point out seats, is nearly as iconic as the building itself.

When Apex was the largest movie theatre chain in the country, responsible for the management of most of Bangkok's first-class cinemas, the Yellow Jackets were a common sight among movie-goers at cinemas across the city. With the Scala now the last remaining branch of a once formidable theatre empire, the beloved Yellow Jackets are the last vestige of the golden age of Bangkok movie palaces. Most of those who remain have been working at the company for decades. For many a regular at the Scala, the faces of the staff are equally as familiar as their flashy outerwear, or the flashy chandelier.

For 50 years, 73-year-old Ubon Klarythong (pictured below), a native of Nakhon Ratchasima province, has been sporting the bright yellow jacket at Scala, having served as cinematic gatekeeper to literally hundreds of thousands of people. "The crowds aren't what they used to be," said Ubon as a screening got underway. "But we have a lot of regulars coming through. I see familiar faces just about everyday. It's almost like having an extended family – Apex is like my family." It's these details, seemingly minor, that are in fact central to solidifying the Scala as a living cultural heritage for Bangkok.

# OPENING NIGHT OF THE OMEN

The 1970s was an inordinately good decade for horror movie fans. The fortuitous combination of loosening social mores and technical innovation in film-making gave the horror film an outsized growth spurt. Films such as William Friedkin's *The Exorcist* and Tobe Hooper's *Texas Chainsaw Massacre* set new standards for the fright factor, albeit in explicitly different directions. Thai audiences were as rapacious a market for horror films as anywhere else. Proof of this can be found on the opening night of Richard Donner's horror classic, *The Omen*, in November 1976. The Thailand premiere of the film went on to be one of the single biggest nights in the history of the Thai movie exhibition industry.

The Apex circuit purchased the distribution rights to *The Omen*, opting for a premiere screening at the Siam theatre in the heart of Siam Square, Bangkok. Intent on maximizing publicity for this latest entry into the horror hall of fame, the company decided on a midnight premiere, hoping to cash in on the heightened fear of the witching hour. Within minutes of the box-office opening the 800-seat theatre was sold out. Extra folding seats were taken out of storage and placed in the aisles and stairwells to help meet demand. But still more people came, crowding the lobby in the hopes of being among the first in Thailand to witness this horror sensation.

As the crowds swelled it became increasingly clear to Siam theatre management that something had to be done if a riot was to be averted. A plan was hatched. Instead of turning away the hordes of latecomers, Apex fired up the projectors at neighboring Lido theatre for a second and simultaneous – albeit staggered – screening. The idea was simple and genius: as the first reel of film completed its cycle at the Siam, it could be swiftly rewound and shuttled over to the Lido. Thus, the same print could be used at two theatres at the same time with a one-reel

time difference between them. When the announcement was made, a tsunami of flailing cinephiles flooded out of Siam's lobby and rushed to the box office at Lido. Cash was thrust frantically through the box-office window, some by crafty ticket scalpers who summarily turned around and resold the tickets at inflated prices to those unwilling to take their chances waiting in line.

By the time the first reel had been completed at the Siam, the Lido, too, was sold out. A seething mass of horror-hungry movie maniacs sat fixated on the screen as the reel was threaded through the projector. Meanwhile, out on Rama 1 road, hundreds more patrons had shown up hoping to nab a ticket now that two theatres were showing the same film. But they were greeted with a "SOLD OUT" sign hanging over the window of both ticket booths. With two reels running simultaneously between the Siam and the Lido, and an ever-growing mob of Omenites pooling outside, there was only one thing left to do.

The third and most luxurious in the Apex-owned trio of Siam Square movie theatres was the Scala. With seating capacity already maxed out at the Siam and Lido, the decision was made to open the Scala for a third simultaneous screening.

In order to pull off this trifecta premiere everything had to run like clockwork. While the third reel was screening at the Siam, the Lido would be on reel number two, and reel number one would be running its course at the Scala. As each reel finished, it was rewound and sent onward to the next theatre, satisfying the movie-watching appetites of over 3,000 cinephiles one reel at one time.

This is perhaps the only time in Thai movie theatre history that a single print of a film served three different movie theatres at the same time. Needless to say, *The Omen* was a hit in Thailand.

# DOUBLE-FEATURE THEATRES

Historically, double-feature theatres served working-class communities. They were the better-value counterpart to the first-class theatres that once peppered central Bangkok with architectural splendour. At the latter, both domestic and foreign films had their Thai premieres, usually unaccompanied by a second feature. Foreign films from Hollywood or Europe were presented with their original language soundtrack (un-dubbed but with Thai subtitles). Once their first run at the downtown movie palaces was complete, the films would circulate to the double-feature theatres where they would be combined in a two-for-one deal with a second film. Any foreign films would then be dubbed over in Thai, making them comprehendible to local audiences.

Double-feature theatres were once a common site throughout metro Bangkok. Some estimate there were close to 100 at their peak. The two-for-one ticket price and stay-all-day policy of double-feature theatres drew steady crowds for many years. For the change in your pocket you could duck the rigours of life with consecutive movies on the silver screen. And if the movie didn't hold your attention then an air-conditioned nap – a luxury for Bangkok's working poor – was the next best thing.

When research for this book started in 2008, there were roughly six double-feature theatres still operating in Bangkok and its suburbs. Most of them were in shabby condition or had gained reputations as flophouses. The last of them went out of business in 2015.

Foyer at the Nakhon Non Rama theatre, Pracharat Road, Nonthaburi.

110

# MONGKOL RAMA THEATRE
## Saphan Khwai, Bangkok
### 1963-2010

Classic International Style architecture characterized the Mongkol Rama theatre, a large double-feature theatre on Phahonyothin Road in the Saphan Khwai neighbourhood of Bangkok. It was erected at a cost of seven million baht in 1963, including the purchase of the land. In those days, the Saphan Khwai area of the city was still mostly rural and had not yet been fully incorporated into urban Bangkok. The theatre was the third constructed by the Panpreecha family as part of their second-run theatre circuit located in neighbourhoods on the outskirts of Bangkok; their other three theatres were the Chalerm Kiad, the Chalerm Sin and the Amornpan. Second generation owner, Fred Panpreecha, closed the Mongkol Rama and sold the property to an office-supply chain, which demolished the building in 2010.

# BANG KHAE RAMA THEATRE
## Bang Khae Market, Bangkok
### 1971-2015

The Bang Khae Rama opened in 1971 in conjunction with a wet market located in front of the theatre. It was part of the Co Brothers' theatre chain, which controlled most of the second-run movie theatres in the Bangkok metropolitan area. Though it didn't close down until 2015, by the late 1980s it had become a porn theatre.

Take a close look to the left of the main entrance where a man can be seen caught in a sprint; I didn't notice him when I was setting up the photo but he appears to be running in order to avoid being photographed while exiting the theatre.

# THONBURI RAMA THEATRE
## Jaransanitwong Road, Bangkok
### 1972-2013

The Thonburi Rama opened as a first-run theatre on 1 February 1972 with Bruce Lee's *The Big Boss*, one of the first major international productions to be filmed in Thailand. The theatre was commissioned by the Cheunpakdee family, which also owned the Ratchathewi Rama. For its first few years it was considered one of the more luxurious theatres on the Thonburi side of Bangkok. By the mid-1970s, however, due to it being located outside of Bangkok's central commercial area, the Thonburi Rama had converted to a second-run theatre, which it remained until it closed in 2013.

# NAKHON NON RAMA THEATRE
## Pracharat Road, Nonthaburi
### 1982-2013

The Nakhon Non Rama theatre was the lone holdout of a business model and structural type once nationwide in scope. The theatre was owned by Surachat Pisitwuthinan, better known by the nickname *Sia* (wealthy Chinese merchant) Hui. Through his movie distribution company, Nakhon Luang Productions, *Sia* Hui once operated a chain of double-feature theatres that stretched throughout Bangkok and included the Sri Krung, the Ngamwongwan and the Sri Siam. Like the Nakhon Non Rama, his theatres were notable for their plush-if-chintzy lobby decor and colourful auditoriums.

ครีเอชั่น® ฉลองปีสตรีสากล แบบเปรี้ยงปร้างครื้นเครง
# แองจี้ ดิ๊คกินส้น
แม่อีหนูตัวแสบ
คมคายสาวป๊ะฉ่าง
ดวงปืนฉะคุยแหลก

EMI

เจียหลิง • เอ่ยจื๋อหยุ่น
ชุยฟู่เชิง • หลิงหลิง
เหลยหมิง

ร่วมด้วย
วิลเลี่ยม แชตาเนอร์
ทอม สเคอร์ริตต์
ซูซาน เซ็นเนตต์
ร็อบบี้ ลี

นิวเฟิร์สต์สตาร์
จัดจำหน่าย โทร. 5110788-5110800

# แม่เสือ
## ปืนกล ธีหนูปืนไว

# อีสาวดี
## The Female Chival

ฉายที่

# WIK KRU THAWEE THEATRE
## Photharam, Ratchaburi province
### 1958-1997

The name Wik Kru Thawee is a composite of the given name and occupation of this theatre's builder and owner, a local school teacher named Thawee Aekarath. *Kru* (teacher) Thawee was passionate about film and viewed the medium as a good way to expand the horizons of the people of Photharam. His love for film was also inherited by his son, Thira Aekarath, who went on to an illustrious career as a cinematographer, best known for shooting the 1970 watershed film *Monrak Luk Thung*.

As far as Thai standalone theatres go, the Wik Kru Thawee comes from an unusual era. It was built in a transitional period for Thai movie theatres, well after concrete had replaced wood as the material of choice but just shy of the nationwide theatre boom that began in 1961.

# CHALERM THONGKHAM THEATRE

## Ban Pong, Ratchaburi province

### 1958-1997

Ban Pong is a junction town. Both the railway and highway fork at Ban Pong, connecting the south with Bangkok to the east and Kanchanaburi to the west. Yet another rail spur heads north towards Suphanburi. Towards the end of World War II, Ban Pong was slated for an aerial bombardment by the Allies as a means of destroying the westbound rail link going towards the border with Burma (now Myanmar). That link, which inspired the movie *Bridge on the River Kwai*, would have enabled the Japanese in Burma to have a supply route from the east. Overcast skies on the bombing day, however, shielded Ban Pong from the bomber's view and the town, with its bustling market area flanking the Mae Klong river and the rail tracks, was spared.

But what war did not do away with, fire did. In 1955, the market area went up in flames, wiping out the densest part of town. Within a few years much of Ban Pong's market area had been rebuilt. The construction was led by a number of wealthy merchants with vested

interests in the area. One of those merchants was Prayun Khotsapongsa, a second-generation Chinese settler whose family owned much of the market. Included in Prayun's redevelopment plan was an enormous, state-of-the-art movie theatre to anchor the surrounding business community. He named the theatre after his mother, Thongkham Wongsarot, and in 1958 the Chalerm Thongkham theatre opened for business.

The growth of the movie industry in Thailand in the post-war years led to healthy competition between theatre operators. Prayun and his family rode the wave of growth by expanding into film distribution. Their company, Chalerm Thongkham Films, distributed films to theatres in eight nearby provinces, including Kanchanaburi, Petchaburi, Suphanburi, Prachuap Khiri Khan, Samut Sakhon, Samut Songkhram and Ratchaburi – Ban Pong's strategic position as a junction town helped make this possible.

In 1958, when the Chalerm Thongkham first opened, movie theatre technology in Thailand was still fairly rudimentary. Ceiling fans were used to cool the theatre and patrons sat on wooden bench seats. By 1967, air-conditioning and bucket seats had been installed, with 800 seats on the lower level and another 300 on the balcony.

Competition stiffened when a new theatre, the Ban Pong Rama, opened on the opposite side of town. To stay competitive, the Khotsapongsa family enlarged the screen to accommodate 70 mm projection capabilities; the large-format film allowed for a bigger, crisper picture, equivalent to the Imax theatres of today.

But, by the close of the 20th century, the Chalerm Thongkham was suffering the typical syndromes that afflicted independent movie theatres across Thailand. Following the Asian financial crisis of 1997, the theatre and distribution company went out of business.

Today, the Chalerm Thongkham theatre houses a motorcycle dealership – a far cry from its glory days as the heart of entertainment in Ban Pong. The building, however, is still a source of pride for the Khotsapongsa family who take pains to ensure that its exterior is maintained with fresh coats of paint and preserved signage.

# PRANBURI RAMA THEATRE
## Pranburi, Prachuap Khiri Khan province
### c. 1980-early 2000s

Located down a narrow residential lane just off the town's main road, the Pranburi Rama theatre closed for business in the early 2000s and was demolished in 2016. Now, Pranburi, like many other Thai towns that once enjoyed a locally-owned theatre, is completely devoid of silver screens.

# BANG SAPHAN NOI THEATRE

## Bang Saphan Noi,
## Prachuap Khiri Khan province
### 1981-early 1990s

The story behind the founding of the Bang Saphan Noi theatre, the first-ever movie theatre to grace the soggy fields of the district it's named for, is a textbook case study of 20th-century Sino-Thai entrepreneurship in rural Thailand.

Starting in the late 19th century, Chinese migration to Thailand was encouraged by successive kings of Thailand's ruling Chakri dynasty. In their push to modernize the country, the Chakri kings invested heavily in canals and, later, trains to open up new land for resource extraction, crop extension and various resulting industries. Chinese immigrants often settled along the canal fronts and train lines, jockeying for position to best capitalize on the new modes of transport. The general pattern was for a first-generation immigrant entrepreneur to set the stage for future capital accumulation and from there the second generation would take the helm. In Bang Saphan Noi, Prayat Phatanaphanich did just that. As he transformed himself from tailor, to cloth merchant, to clothier, to land owner and to coconut plantation owner, he used the profits from one enterprise to reinvest in others, diversifying revenue streams and often resulting in little local empires. By the early 1980s, the Phatanaphanich family was an established business family in town. Like much of rural Thailand at the time, Bang Saphan Noi did not yet have widespread electricity and only the well-heeled could afford such a luxury. As a result, demand for post-work leisure activity was high.

To meet that need, Prayat and a few other investors built the Bang Saphan Noi theatre in 1981. The theatre was erected on land adjacent to Prayat's coconut plantation and he used another neighbouring plot for the construction of a Chinese temple and to house his numerous relatives and employees, some of whom worked in the theatre. The theatre closed down in the early 1990s. Today it stands as a vacant ruin and marker of a culturally richer time.

# KHOSIT THEATRE
## Ban Pong, Ratchaburi province
### 1983-2002

Although the most highly-touted architectural works in Thailand tend to relate to the dominant national narrative – generally either royalty or religion – there is a wide range of world-class work outside of that scope. Modern architecture, in particular, is especially well-represented throughout Thailand. Most Thai towns are largely comprised of various offshoots of that broadly defined school known as the International Style. Though much of it is rather plain in both proportion and dimension, there are truly outstanding pieces all around, some of them tucked away in the most obscure places. Ban Pong's Khosit theatre falls into that category: outstanding obscura – forgotten but unique modern Thai architecture.

What is it about the Khosit that makes it so architecturally special? For one, you seldom see buildings with this kind of top-heavy massing. The brutally heavy upper bulk seems to float weightlessly over the empty lower lobby and from ground level it appears as if the foundation was raised up and left suspended in the air. The contrast between the bulky top and empty bottom is tied together by a wrap-around marquee and a strip of windows between the two. The marquee protrudes out around the edges while the windows are set back. Add some asymmetry to the package, along with a softly curved corner (to lessen the severity of the bulk) and the Khosit stands out as a highly sophisticated structure. The roof-top signage, moreover, with the lettering done on large squares of metal, matches the bulkiness below.

ภาพยนตร์วิทยาศาสตร์ก้าวหน้ายุค 20 ศตวรรษ
สงคราม
ใต้บาดาล
มหัศจรรย์
เรื่องพิเศษยิ่งใหญ่ของ โตโฮ
โตโฮ สโคป
สีอีสต์แมน
船大決鬥
TEL. 212787
การภาพยนตร์ฮอลลีวู้ด ยกย่องเป็นบรมครู ได้ฝากฝีมือให้วงการภาพยนตร์ทั่วโลกต้องตื่นตลึงเป็นเรื่องสุดท้าย ก่อนจบชีวิต
แค๊ปปิตอลฟิล์ม
จัดจำหน่าย
พูดภาษาอังกฤษในฟิล์ม
บรรยาย ไทย • จีน
วันที่
เดือน

# LUNA THEATRE

## Yala

### 1960-mid-1990s

The Luna theatre was built in 1960 at the height of the International Style movement in architecture. It stayed in business until the mid-1990s, after which its auditorium was gutted and turned into a parking garage; nothing therein remains that is worthy of documentation. Fortunately, parts of the lobby were spared the hatchet and the decorative details are still visible to all who enter. In particular, the right lower lobby and accompanying staircase (pictured left), which once led movie-goers up to balcony seating, are fairly well-preserved. If this colourful sliver is any indicator, the Luna must once have been a sight to behold – the facade is pictured above in its 1960s heyday.

# SIAM THEATRE
## Yala
### 1961-1992

Geographically speaking, the Siam theatre feels like the centre of Yala, and not just the centre of the old commercial core (where it is located), but the centre of the entire province. It is almost as if the old mandala system of Buddhist monarchical rule in Yala fanned outwards from its cosmological core at the Siam theatre; if only in name, that's not such a stretch of the imagination as the theatre was originally called the King's Theatre. With its terminated vista anchoring the middle of old downtown, the Siam is a spectacle even now that it is no longer operational. It is pictured here in its heyday in 1971 (right) and with bricked up windows today (below).

# PETCH RAMA
## Trang
### 1978-1995

The Petch Rama stands in the centre of Trang city, the original anchor for a now rundown commercial plaza. The narrowness of the plaza makes it difficult to get a good view of this striking piece of modernist architecture from street level. I had to convince the proprietor of a noodle shop located opposite to allow me on the roof of his establishment in order to photograph the full scale of the theatre.

Despite its handsome facade, the Petch Rama is an utter ruin. The roof has been removed, allowing the interior to be completely exposed to the elements. Trees grow where snack kiosks once stood. A family of dogs dwells under the seating level. It would be a miracle if this building were to be salvaged from the almost certain throes of death.

# PARADISE THEATRE

## Pattani

### 1981-2006

Of the five movie theatres that have served Pattani over the years, the Paradise theatre is the only one remaining that has any resemblance to its original function. Unsurprisingly, the Paradise was the most recently built of all the city's theatres. It dates only to 1981, the tail end of Thailand's standalone movie-theatre construction boom. Its most recent owner, the southern Thai movie producer and director, Khom Akaradej, closed it down in 2006, not long after the southern insurgency began impacting the city.

While the Paradise's dimensional signage still sits boldly atop the cornice, gently reminding people of merrier times, the once cavernous auditorium has become home to swiftlets.

# Chapter 3
## THE LATECOMERS
## OF ISAN

Of all Thailand's five regions, only Isan – the northeast part of the country – has experienced growth in the number of standalone movie theatres since Thailand's movie theatre construction boom (1961-1981). Though this phenomenon has not extended much into the 21st century, it is a stark contradiction to what has happened in other parts of the country. The reasons are complex but there are two main components: one is related directly to the domestic film distribution industry, the other is a byproduct of Isan's relationship with the rest of Thailand.

Isan is one of the least geographically integrated parts of the country. Culturally and linguistically it tends to have more in common with Laos than the rest of Thailand. Geographical disconnect, combined with the highest rate of household poverty in the country has made the region less attractive for outside investors. Until the early 2010s, this held true for the nationwide theatre chains as well. The result was that local theatre operators in Isan were insulated from the capital-heavy competition out of Bangkok. Single-screen theatres in small towns and provincial capitals were thus able to retain enough of a movie-going market to stay in business.

As for the film distribution component, Isan has a unique situation which makes it less prone to monopolization than other parts of the country; three different companies have distribution rights in Isan. In other regions of the country, a lone distributor has exclusive control over which movies play at which theatres resulting in theatre operators having less say over their content, not to mention unfavourable revenue-sharing schemes.

For these reasons, a handful of standalone theatres have been built in Isan over the past two decades. Although two of them have since gone out of business, the trend represents a welcome anachronism in the movie theatre industry. These theatres also represent the only remaining operational standalone movie theatres in Thailand outside of Bangkok.

**Previous pages:** Rolling credits at the Sri Pong Cineplex, Phimai, Nakhon Ratchasima province.
**Opposite:** The Det Udom Mini theatre, Ubon Ratchathani.

# PRINCE CINEPLEX
## Kalasin
### 1972-2013

When it was built in the early 1970s under the name Kalasin Rama, the Prince Cineplex had a single, enormous screen and a seating capacity in the range of one thousand. In the late 1990s, the Khon Kaen-based Prince Cinema chain purchased the old Kalasin Rama and turned its giant auditorium into two smaller ones (a procedure known as 'twinning'), which allowed them to diversify the film fare shown at any given time and attract a wider audience.

As the new and improved Prince Cineplex boomed, it siphoned ticket sales from other Kalasin theatres, including the older, smaller but much prettier Lak Mueang theatre. When questioned about why an elegant theatre like the Lak Mueang had gone out of business, the manager of the Prince Cineplex responded glibly, "Because of us."

The Prince Cineplex itself went out of business in 2013, shortly after one of the two national chains opened a multiplex in town.

# DET UDOM MINI THEATRE
## Det Udom, Ubon Ratchathani province
### 1990-present day

The Det Udom Mini Theatre is one of the last few standalone movie theatres to be built in Thailand. It replaced an old wooden theatre that had previously occupied the same plot. While typologically a standalone theatre, the Det Udom Mini is a 'twin' theatre, meaning it was designed with two auditoriums and two screens so that two movies can be shown simultaneously.

In past decades, country theatres like the Det Udom Mini could be found in nearly every district of Thailand. Even prior to the advent of rural electrification, small town entrepreneurs were known for building movie theatres and powering them with the aid of diesel generators. Areas deemed too poor or remote to support a permanent theatre were serviced by the ubiquitous travelling cinema companies, which would set up open-air movie screenings and charge customers a small fee per view.

The people of Det Udom, however, have long been luxuriating in a theatre of their own. As of this writing, the Det Udom Mini theatre is one of only three standalone movie theatres still operating in all of Thailand.

# CHUM PHAE CINEPLEX
## Chum Phae, Khon Kaen province
### 2001-present day

Like the Chum Phae Cineplex, a large portion of Thai standalone movie theatres are set back in courts, plazas, or otherwise removed from the main road. Although the space in front is often used by movie-goers to park their motorbikes, the distance between theatre and thoroughfare serves as insulation against noise and pollution. As public space is painfully absent in most Thai urban areas, a downtown cinema with an open-air lobby is almost akin to a park.

The term 'cineplex', when applied to a single-screen standalone movie theatre is a little misleading. Breaking the compounded word in two we are left with 'cinema' and 'complex', which implies a plurality of parts. Conventionally speaking, a cineplex will either have more than one screen or more than one function. But in the case of many late-era Thai standalones, of which there are only a few, the term is applied for strictly semantic reasons. Cineplex sounds more up to date and more fashionably modern than the traditional terms 'cinema', 'theatre', or, in the Thai lexicon, 'rama'. Still the Chum Phae Cineplex is, in actuality, a standalone.

# SRI PONG CINEPLEX
## Phimai, Nakhon Ratchasima province
## 2005-2018

The Sri Pong was a second-generation movie theatre. Constructed in 2005, it replaced an old wooden theatre that dated to the 1950s and was in grave disrepair. Instead of bowing out of the theatre business and using the land for some alternative purpose, the proprietary family built anew and named the new theatre after the deceased father-cum-founder of its wooden predecessor, Pong. The Sri Pong Cineplex provided first-class entertainment for Phimai until it went out of business in May 2018, making it one of the last operating standalone movie theatres in the country.

# Chapter 4

# OVER THE MEKONG: LAOS

On the opposite bank of the Mekong river, Laos has had an equally variegated if not nearly as prolific movie theatre history as Thailand. The long riparian partition that comprises most of the Thai-Lao border has even helped to facilitate filmic exchanges, with reels of film moving back and forth to fill market demand as needed.

Though largely imbalanced in favour of cinema exports from Thailand to Laos, an elderly theatre owner in Nong Khai, Thailand, claimed that the earliest films to reach her remote Isan province arrived not from Bangkok as might be expected, but from Laos. It's interesting to speculate what route these films might have taken to reach Isan: they may have come via Vietnam or Cambodia, perhaps carried by an itinerant French merchant, and arrived in Isan by way of a trans-Laotian trade route; they may have first been screened in the royal Lao capital of Luang Prabang and then sailed down the Mekong to secondary port cities bound together through age-old trading networks; or they may even have come overland all the way from China. Whatever the answer, by the 1950s, the flow of films from Laos to Thailand had reversed course.

No more than a handful of commercial Lao films were ever made, and even fewer of them were screened in Thai theatres, but that didn't mean movie-going was any less popular in Laos than in Thailand. Movie theatres, some rivalling or even surpassing the comfort offered by those across the Mekong, sprang up in all of the larger towns in Laos. In the years after French decolonization

**Previous pages:** Tolaphap theatre, Xiengkhouang.
**Left:** Discarded furniture in the lobby of the Lao Chaleun theatre, Savannakhet.

and before the ascension of the communist Pathet Lao government – an era defined in large measure by the Laotian Civil War – films were routinely exported from Thailand to Laos for exhibition in Lao movie theatres. Linguistic and cultural similarities made Thai films an easy sell among Lao movie-goers, with stars such as Mitr Chaibancha and Sombath Methanee becoming household names throughout the country. American involvement in the Laotian Civil War guaranteed Hollywood films a major role in Lao theatres, but Hollywood did not have a monopoly. French cinema in particular enjoyed privileged status in Lao theatres due to the relatively high number of Francophones in the country.

Meanwhile, in the remote northeastern provinces of Houaphan and Phongsali, a markedly different kind of cinema was being screened. The communist Pathet Lao and their North Vietnamese allies had taken control of these provinces as early as 1955. Film was used as part of a propaganda effort to attract recruits and foment rebellion against the Royal Lao Government and their American backers. In one of the more famous cases, a theatre was set up within the Vieng Xai cave complex in Houaphan province, where local cadre screened anti-western, anti-royal propaganda films while in hiding during American carpet-bombing campaigns. (All known movie theatres in this area had been demolished before research for this book commenced.)

After the defeat of the Royal Lao Government at the hands of the Pathet Lao, movie theatres were nationalized and the movies screened went through a drastic change. Films from countries in the American sphere of Cold War influence were banned, while Soviet, North Korean, Vietnamese and Indian films took their place.

Movie-theatre construction, though very limited, continued into the communist era thanks to assistance from Soviet and Vietnamese allies. The few remaining theatres in Laos were built during the tumultuous years of the Laotian Civil War or shortly thereafter. None of them, however, are currently operating. After the collapse of the Soviet Union – the main patron of the Lao People's Democratic Republic – the funds necessary to keep the theatres running were cut off. By the mid-1990s, not a single theatre in the entire country was active on a full-time basis.

## FOND MEMORIES OF LAO CINEMA

A former Lao national living in France since 1975 recalls the Odeon Rama theatre in Vientiane:

"I don't remember exactly when the Odeon Rama opened, but it was the last theatre built in Vientiane in the late sixties or early seventies. I used to live nearby. It was the biggest and most beautiful theatre in town, with comfy, red velvet seats. Like all countries in Southeast Asia at that time, Indian and Chinese movies were popular among the local people. It was there that I discovered Bruce Lee, Bollywood and my favourite of all, the Monkey King movies, based on the classical Chinese novel *Journey to the West*. They also played some Thai movies. I remember one night when my parents brought me to see a French comedy starring Yves Montand and Louis de Funès. The atmosphere was strange to me that night. The theatre was full of French people. It was the first time that I saw such a place filled with Europeans; so many white faces in one room. That night, the Odeon Rama was transformed into a movie theatre near Place de l'Odeon in Paris."

# LAO CHALEUN THEATRE
## Savannakhet
### c. 1930s-1980s

The Lao Chaleun theatre must have been considered a mega-project for sleepy Savannakhet when it was erected in the 1930s. The complex comprises almost an entire city block, including two rows of commercial and residential buildings in addition to a massive cinema hall. The theatre itself is divided into two separate sections. The facade and facilities attached to it face onto Kaysone Phomvihane Road, while the main auditorium is in another building in a back alley. A long corridor leads from the front entrance to the auditorium in the rear and the two sections are connected by a patio bridge. Despite being in a state of utter disrepair, the Lao Chaleun is one of the city's key landmarks; a 1930s tropical art deco masterpiece, palatial in size, with an inviting, carnival-like beauty.

# VIENG SAMAY THEATRE
## Vientiane
### 1957-1975

The Vieng Samay theatre dates to the late 1950s and is a legacy of the first years of American economic and technical 'assistance' to Laos during the Cold War era. As a palimpsest on Vientiane's urban landscape, it is a critical piece of the city's social past, one that certainly adds architectural and historical capital to an already varied urban tapestry. Sadly, nobody else saw it that way. This once popular movie theatre was demolished in 2016 and, as of this writing, the plot it stood on was being used as a parking lot.

# SIEN SAVAN THEATRE
## Luang Prabang
### 1962-1993

Much like the city it stands in, one would be hard pressed to find a movie theatre with more quaint charm than the Sien Savan. Built in late 1962 by a Chinese-Lao family, the Sien Savan was the first brick-and-mortar theatre in the former royal capital. Like all movie theatres in Laos, the Sien Savan was partially nationalized after 1975, coming under the direction of the Ministry of Culture, which amounted to a sharing arrangement between the original owners and the government's Department of Cinema.

While movies from Thailand, France and the United States were banned from Lao silver screens, replacements were brought in from communist ally countries like Vietnam, Russia and non-aligned India. Films from communist China were absent from the film fare due to poor relations between the two countries; the Lao People's Party had been under the tutelage of the Vietnamese, who had shifted political allegiance from China to the Soviet Union.

The Sien Savan has been closed since the early 1990s. For a brief period, it was turned into a restaurant, hoping to capitalize on the influx of tourists that Luang Prabang has received since it gained UNESCO World Heritage status. As of this writing there are murmurs that it will someday be brought back to life in conjunction with the Luang Prabang Film Festival.

# SENO RAMA THEATRE
## Seno, Savannakhet province
### 1970-1991

Seno has long been home to a military base, dating back to the days of French imperialism. Even prior to that, Seno had geostrategic importance due to its position at a vital north-south and east-west junction. When the Seno Rama theatre opened in 1970, the nearby military base was home to battalions of the Royal Lao Army. Salaried soldiers, in dire need of peril-relieving escapism in the days before television became widespread, represented a reliable clientele for a movie theatre proprietor. And so, with a built-in market in mind, the Seno Rama was erected at the height of the Laotian Civil War. Today the theatre has been repurposed as a badminton hall.

# NANG LIT THEATRE
## Savannakhet
### c. 1970-1994 (reopened 2011-2014)

Half a block from the Lao Chaleun on the opposite side of the road stands the Nang Lit theatre. Dating to around 1970, it was built in place of a much older wooden theatre that once stood on the same ground. The original owner, a Laotian of Chinese descent, named the theatre after his daughter, Lit, and operated it in stiff competition with three other theatres that once vied for the patronage of Savannakhet's entertainment seekers.

In the wake of Pathet Lao ascendancy in May 1975, the owner and his family crossed over into Thailand en route to refuge in the United States, forever relinquishing their cinema when it was seized by the communist regime. To this day, it is easily one of the most striking buildings ever to grace Savannakhet's gridded streets.

In 2011, a private exhibitor leased the building, renaming it the Khounsavan Cinema. It was unable to draw enough of an audience to stay in business and closed again in 2014 although it is occasionally used for private events.

# THE LAO-VIET CULTURAL HALL OF FRIENDSHIP

## Oudomxay

### 1981-1991

A banner above the stage at the Lao-Viet Cultural Hall of Friendship proclaims, "Long live the Lao People's Democratic Republic." Directly beneath, another reads, "Long live the glory of the Lao People's Revolutionary Party." While both the Republic and the Party are alive and well today, the Lao-Viet Cultural Hall of Friendship is no more.

The hall was a gift from the communist Vietnamese government to their Lao comrades in the city of Oudomxay. Much like the French giving the Statue of Liberty to the Americans, it was built as an act of political diplomacy – in movie theatre form.

This testament to late Soviet-era functionalist design was built in 1981, six years after the triumph of the Lao communists over the American-backed royalist government and at the height of the country's short-lived experiment with a centrally-planned economy. By 1986, the commune system had been completely abandoned on the heels of 'big brother' Vietnam's switch to a market economy.

Outside of Vientiane and a few of the larger cities in Laos, the country never saw much in the way of socialist architecture. In 2012, one of its finest examples in the north of the country – the Lao-Viet Cultural Hall of Friendship – was demolished for a new building with no connection to cinema.

ฉลอง ภักดีวิจิตร
กำกับการแสดง

บางกอกการภาพยนตร์
BANGKOK FILM CO.,LTD.

Chapter 5

BEHIND THE SCENES

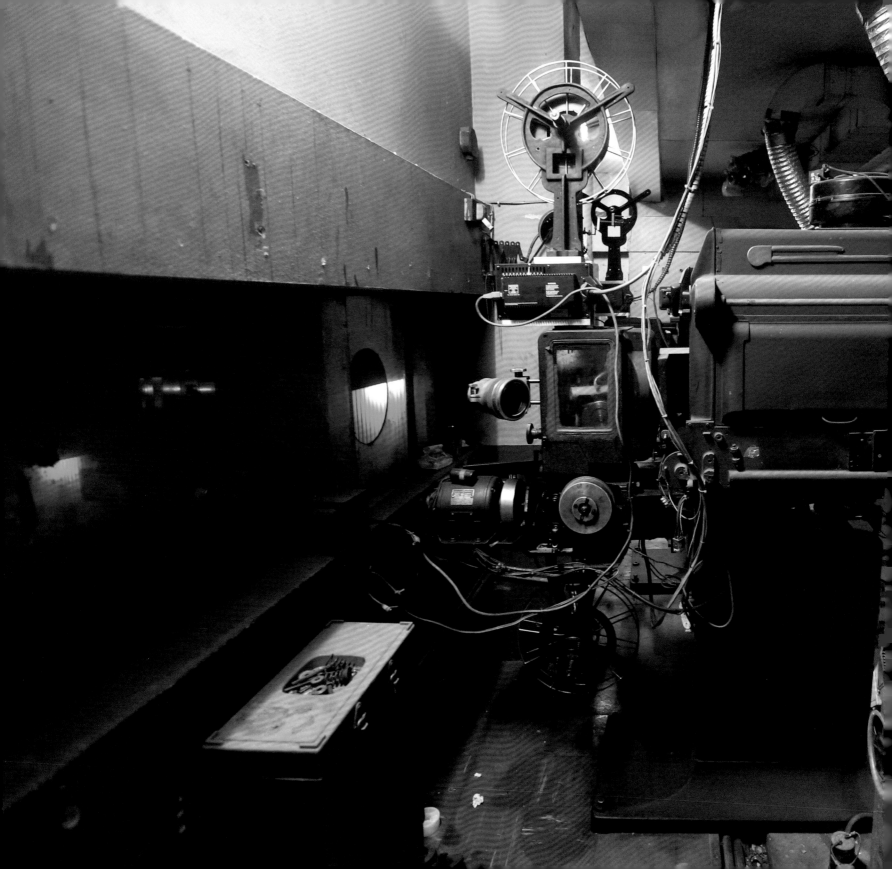

# INSIDE THE BOOTH

In the context of cinema, the phrase 'the show must go on' would be moot without the projectionist. Who else would know how to thread the film (in the days of film), spark the carbon rod (in the days of carbon-arc projectors) and time the changeover so that it picks up exactly where the previous reel left off?

There is a Quasimodo quality to the projectionist's trade. Much like the fictional French bell ringer, the projectionist is a phantom worker – an anonymous, often solitary, toiler stationed outside and above a cavernous sanctuary filled with the devoted. They are the least visible but most indispensable members of the movie-theatre guild. Nobody in the crowd gives them a thought until something goes wrong with the picture or audio, at which point the projectionist is transmogrified into the loathed hunchback up above. For a flawless screening, the projectionist receives no praise.

During the boom era of the standalone movie theatre, most Thai theatres were equipped with American-made reel-to-reel, carbon-arc projectors, a technology named after the sparkler-like rods that provided the light source. Unlike the automated digital projectors common in today's movie theatres, carbon-arc projectors required careful monitoring. As the rods burn down the mirror that reflects the light onto the screen needs to be adjusted lest the picture's brightness fluctuate. A single 20-minute reel of film needs at least four inches of carbon rod to run its full cycle. A careless projectionist could very easily cause silver screen mayhem.

By the 1970s, most of the world's movie theatres had switched over to using xenon bulb projectors, doing away with the higher maintenance carbon arcs. This xenon-bulb revolution, while not eliminating the need for technically-savvy projectionists, greatly reduced their work load and made it much easier for a single person to monitor two projectors at the same time. But the xenon-bulb revolution did not reach most Thai movie theatres until the late 1980s, roughly the same time that standalone theatres in Thailand started losing money. Rather than make the costly transition from carbon arc to xenon bulb, many theatre owners opted to close up shop. Projectionists employed at the few standalone theatres that survived into the 21st century had to be cavalier technicians, often working with decades-old projectors that required constant attention. At the twilight of the standalone era, the craft of the skilled projectionist was similarly on the brink of extinction.

# A PROJECTIONIST AT WORK

Amnuay is a veteran projectionist – a true old hand. He got his start as the projectionist at the Sri Surin theatre in neighbouring Surin province before moving to the Sisaket Rama in the provincial capital. Both theatres are now out of business. A decade has gone by since he got his third gig as projectionist at the Thai Rama theatre in Uthumphon Phisai. Notwithstanding a miracle, there won't be another chance to practice his craft should this gig expire.

The Thai Rama is a bastion of family entertainment in small-town Isan. The owner's rock-bottom entrance fee of 20 baht is the lowest in the country, making the big screen accessible for even the most pecuniary viewer. In the second decade of the 21st century, an active standalone theatre in rural Thailand is an anachronism.

Amnuay (pictured on page 163, and overleaf) mans a clunky two-reel changeover projection system that could be in a museum. It's at least as old as the theatre itself, which dates to 1977; in the working life of projection equipment, that's grandmotherly. Only with a lot of extra tweaking and coddling are these machines able to perform their job.

A cacophony of motors sets an industrial mood in the projection room. Antiquated projectors require hawkish attention. At times they cause the on-screen picture to shake – the result of a loose imaging lens. The audio system fails on occasion, too, leaving the audience of 20 or so in awkward silence. The amount of attention required just to ensure a steady picture and an even light source is praiseworthy. This is no mindless task; tedious, yes, but not unskilled. When one reel has nearly finished, Amnuay switches on the other projector. The so-called 'changeover' system staying true to its name, the expired reel is then removed and taken to an adjacent room where it is rewound by hand.

The rewinding bit has a meditative quality. In the minute or two it takes Amnuay to complete a reel he seems lost in thought, watching as the film shrinks from one reel only to grow, correspondingly, into a tightly wound circle on the other. Occasionally he glances out of the wall opening towards the distant screen, checking that the film is playing smoothly in his absence.

Above the wall opening hang portraits of the late King Bhumibol and Queen Sirikit. Most businesses in Thailand keep images of royalty prominently displayed. The portraits on display in the Thai Rama are

inscribed with blessings of good luck and prosperity, and have presided over this room since the cinema opened.

While the projectors hum away, clamorous in their melody, Amnuay reads the newspaper – a solitary moment, his machines clanking in the background. Moments like these make up the completion of a reel cycle and several minutes pass this way before he returns to the machine to adjust its components. It takes about five or six reels to complete a typical feature film.

Not too long ago, the theatre was full on a regular basis. The Thai Rama had an original seating capacity of 1,000. Now only 200 seats remain, the rest sold off as scrap. The projectors in this steamy little room are aged artifacts. When they go, so will the theatre. Projectionists like Amnuay are like members of a fading guild. To see their occupation still in action at this particular point in time is to watch occupational Darwinism unfold before your very eyes. A sterile silence awaits this room where dreams have been projected twice a day since 1977. On considering this fact, Amnuay shrugs and cracks a smile before loading another reel.

* Since this was written, the Thai Rama theatre has gone out of business and been demolished.

# GLASS-SLIDE ADVERTISEMENTS

When independently-owned standalone movie theatres were the norm in Thailand, theatres served as advertising conduits for local businesses, generating a bit of additional income for the movie houses in the process. This was accomplished within the theatre itself, where advertisements were projected onto the screen before the start of a film. While this technique is still common in theatres today, the method for doing so in bygone eras was quite different.

Until the 1980s in Thailand, advertisements were produced on glass slides, which were then projected onto the screen via a magic lantern slide projector. At any given theatre, particularly those in smaller towns, ads were primarily for nearby businesses, many of which were often within walking distance of the movie theatre itself. Major brands and national chains also advertised at local theatres, especially if their product was carried at a local store or the company had a nearby branch.

During elections, political candidates often advertised at the local theatre via glass slide. Public service announcements were likewise commonly featured. The second slide on the right was salvaged from a theatre in central Thailand and shows a cartoonish character that looks like a police officer standing contemplatively in front of his rural bamboo hut with a thought bubble containing Bangkok's Democracy Monument and the words, "Must go vote on 13 September."

THE DUBBERS

# VOICES BEHIND THE ACTION

There are few figures more central to the blossoming of Thailand's movie exhibition industry than the live dubber. For decades, these crafty voice actors were the heart and soul of the movie-going experience, performing unique spoken interpretations of characters in both foreign and Thai films from a boxy little room beside the projection booth. Popular dubbers could sell out a movie theatre based on their name alone, rivalling the top actors of the day for star power.

While it was the coupling of live dubbing with motion picture that brought fame to the profession, the groundwork for the art form to flourish was already long established thanks to the traditional Sanskritic drama that had made its way into Thailand from India via the Malay world in the 19th century. A common feature of these dramatic performances was the frequent and spontaneous interaction of the actors with the audience, which gave the latter a sense of being part of the show. When film overtook live performance as the Thai public's entertainment medium of choice, movie dubbers simply continued this interactive tradition.

From the very earliest days of movie theatres in Thailand voice actors played a critical role. During the silent film era, a sort of proto-dubber was hired to read aloud the intertitles to the crowd. After World War II the dubbing profession came into its own, solidifying its place in the theatre just as the Thai film industry was itself beginning to bloom. Soon after the war, new film-making technologies imported from countries across the industrialized world began making their way to Thailand at prices that were accessible to a larger market than ever before; a result of post-war political and trade realignments. Motion picture cameras, film splicers, projectors and sound systems, as well as

many other implements of the craft, all found their way to specialty shops clustered around the Sala Chalerm Krung theatre in central Bangkok in what was essentially the movie and movie-theatre supply district for the entire country. Better access to equipment gave rise to an increase in film making. Yet, in spite of these technological advances, film producers kept a tight fist on movie budgets. As such, the preferred format for shooting a movie was on 16 mm film, which produced a richly coloured picture but lacked sound-recording capabilities. This necessitated the rise of live movie dubbers to perform the voices – as well as the sound effects – for this new wave of Thai cinema.

Live dubbing gave the films an immediacy that Thai audiences grew fond of, echoing the interactive nature of Sanskritic performance that older generations were accustomed to. For much of the post-war period, dubbed Thai films competed briskly with blockbusters from Hollywood and elsewhere. It wasn't until the early 1970s that the 16 mm era tapered off, giving way to sound films shot on 35 mm for which voice actors were unnecessary. But instead of fading away, the dubbing profession forged ahead thanks to the large number of foreign films imported by Thailand's distributors and movie theatre owners.

It was in this translational context that the talents of a good dubber became most attractive to Thai audiences. For foreign films in particular, the key to winning over the crowd as a dubber was the ability to improvise on the spot, tweak the characters or even the plot to make it slightly more relevant to the local audience. For instance, if the dubber was from the same town or region where a theatre was located, he or she might speak in the local dialect, or even adapt characters in the film to represent local personalities.

Well-known dubbers Sirichai Duangphatra (left) and Toh Panthamit (right), circa 1980s.

# SIRICHAI'S SERPICO

The year was 1973, a particularly volatile year in Thai history remembered for large-scale student protests against a corrupt, dictatorial regime and the violent military crackdown that ended them. Into this context of heightened political tension, with the flames of people power burning hot, Sidney Lumet's iconic police drama *Serpico*, starring the wildly popular Al Pacino in the title role, opened at the Indra theatre in Nakhon Si Thammarat.

*Serpico* is the Hollywood account of real-life New York city cop Frank Serpico's political lynching at the hands of the New York Police Department. In the film, as in real life, the upstanding cop refused to take kickbacks from local criminal organizations, as was common among many in the NYPD at the time. By shunning the practice and serving as a whistle blower against police corruption in general, Frank Serpico drew the wrath of the entire New York police bureaucracy, almost getting himself killed in the process.

Nakhon Si Thammarat in the early 1970s had a similar problem with its own police force. Many officers had acquired a base reputation for corruption, extortion and other forms of constabulary graft. Local grievances against the police were high, so when *Serpico* made its premiere at the Indra theatre sympathetic crowds showed up in droves.

Among Nakhon Si Thammarat's more famous dubbers of the time was a man named Sirichai Duangphatra (pictured opposite), who was, by all accounts, a master at rousing a crowd. Whether the movie was foreign or Thai, Sirichai always reserved his southern Thai accent for sidekicks and supporting characters, much to the amusement of the southern Thai audience. But Sirichai's greatest talent was his deft ability to modify a film's plot and characters to sync with contemporary Thai issues. He had a penchant, moreover, for using his role as dubber to address the day's top political scandals, both at the national and local level. And corrupt politicians were his number one target. With *Serpico*, making political satire for Sirichai was like shooting fish in a barrel; it turned out to be his voice-over magnum opus.

The crooked cops in the film were all given names corresponding to Nakhon Si Thammarat's most notorious lawmen. The crowd, well aware of who was who among the police ne'er-do-wells, reacted with cheers and hysterical laughter. The on-screen cops and the cops on the streets of Nakhon Si Thammarat, if only for a few hours, became one and the same in the eyes and ears of Indra theatre patrons. From the rank-and-file right up to the top brass, no corrupt member of the local police department was spared Sirichai's adaptive lampoonery. The crowd went wild and because the film's initial dubbing session was recorded on tape for use in later screenings, multiple crowds were exposed to Sirichai's crusades.

Not everybody got a kick out of Sirichai's antics, however, and his satirical *Serpico* adaptation got him slapped with a libel lawsuit. Though he ended up being found guilty, the incrimination martyred him, making him into a local hero and even more popular among movie-goers in Nakhon Si Thammarat.

Sirichai's career as a movie dubber came to a close with the decline of Nakhon Si Thammarat's standalone movie theatres, as it did for all of Thailand's once illustrious voice actors. For Sirichai, the experience gained working a crowd of movie-goers was parlayed into a career in politics, though he died prematurely before his political career had a chance to take off.

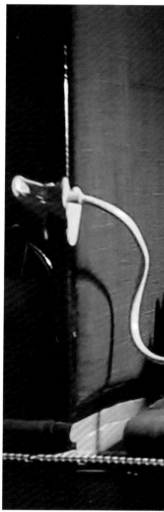

Like many other aspects of the movie exhibition industry, the decline of the standalone movie theatre in Thailand marked a similar decline in live dubbing. As the need for the art form in live settings faded out so did the vast majority of those who made a career from it. Among those who successfully transitioned to studio dubbing was a baritone from Hat Yai named Pariphan Vacharanon, better known by his stage name Toh Panthamit. Over the years, Toh and his team of voice actors (pictured left, with Toh on the far left) have become some of the most recognizable voices in Thai entertainment, responsible for providing voices for most of the larger international productions distributed to Thailand. From their humble studio in Nonthaburi province, where they churn out dozens of hours of recordings per week, their voices have been heard by the majority of people in Thailand.

"Back when I was still performing live, I did a session at the Petch Rangsit theatre," says Toh, who was not deterred by the low wages and long hours of his profession. "The owner was a very kind man, but the theatre was known for showing triple features. It was a second-run theatre, so they could screen films all day. I did the voices for three movies in a row, along with my female counterpart. Very tiring. In those days, that was what life was like for us dubbers. We didn't make a lot of money. I was paid 250 baht for three films in a row. But when you work a job for the love of it, that's how it is."

The Painters

Traditionally, movie posters serve as the link between film and movie theatres. As an advertising medium they are meant to convey all the necessary information about a film while requiring minimum time and effort from the viewer. That logic, however, doesn't necessarily apply to the movie posters of Thailand. Beginning in the early 1960s, Thai movie poster artists turned the medium on its head, moving away from the increasingly streamlined style that was gaining traction in many other parts of the world towards a more frenetic look.

The Thai masters began the practice of enhancing poster art, filling each work with hand-painted imagery often copied directly from lobby cards and other promotional materials sent to theatres in advance of a film. Most painters enlarged their contents via the grid method, a technique that involves drawing a grid over the source material and copying it, square by square, into a corresponding grid drawn on a blank billboard many times larger. This method ensured the most accurate recreation of detail. Others artists painted freehand, allowing for spontaneity. Either way, the result was eye-catching; a blitz of hand-painted colour that in today's insta-sharing world would be sure to multiply the viewership of these original works in a viral flurry.

The father of this edgy new style was Somboonsuk Niyomsiri, better known by his alias Piak Poster. He drew on the minimalist trends of early 1960s movie poster art in the west (think Saul Bass, the graphic designer who defined Hollywood title font and poster art of the day) and proceeded to ramp up the art form by doubling down on details. A typical work produced at his studio blended a background of 1960s psychedelic art with a foreground consisting of a central figure interlaced with scenes and lesser characters from the film. It was provocative work that created a collage of action which could either be taken in at a glance or enjoyed at length. This style would come to define Thai poster art for the next 30 years as Piak Poster's understudies such as Suchin Pansamut, Banhan Thaithonboon and the legendary Tongdee Panumas furthered the techniques he pioneered.

Piak Poster's artistic innovations were not developed on a whim, nor were the movie distribution companies that hired the artists out to blindly subsidize their vivid craft. Behind the spectacle was sound logic rooted in the theatre boom of the early 1960s. As access to movie theatres increased for millions of Thais living in remote and rural areas, movie posters (which, after all, are just glorified advertisements) were in need of bending to this voluminous new market. The artwork had to be direct, explicit and visually intelligible to a population for whom formal education was often low and illiteracy high. Movie audiences usually based their decision

**Left:** Billboard painter at work, circa 1960s.
**Opposite:** A double billing at the Baworn theatre, Nakhon Phanom, features a Chinese action flick and an American comedy western, 1969.

Mobile advertising for a double billing at the President theatre, Songkhla, with poster art signed by Piak Poster.

to watch a particular film as much on the quality of the poster art as on the movie's cast. As one Bangkok poster dealer recalled, "Kids growing up in Isan didn't have access to information about movies that were playing. We would make our decisions based on the artwork of the movie posters. If a poster looked interesting, we'd go watch the movie. If it didn't catch our attention we would pass." So, while poster art in the industrialized countries of the world was evolving towards more abstract compositions, in Thailand, it was going baroque with an outsized appeal aimed at the senses – romance, violence and all.

During the golden age of this art form, from the 1960s through the early '80s, any given movie theatre had at least one painter on the payroll. In some cases, the artists took up full-time residency within the theatres, sleeping in rooms built expressly to house them

and the implements of their craft. In Bangkok, where multiple theatres competed for a finite number of movie-goers, billboard production took on an industrial quality with warehouse-sized studios employing gangs of artists to create the most stunning representations in the largest size possible.

The most impressive movie advertisements were often giant, hand-crafted cut-outs featuring characters, or even settings, from films. The effect was a splash of dimensionality that made the works pop. Some of the flashier illustrations were reserved for the back of pick-up trucks, which were towed through the streets to maximize viewership. A pre-recorded announcement for the film was piped through megaphones on the trucks, drawing further attention to these mobile movie ads.

By 1990, the era of hand-painted movie posters in Thailand was

Mobile poster art for Hong Kong kung fu film *Lethal Panther*, directed by Godfrey Ho, 1991.

rapidly winding down. In an effort to cut costs, distributors turned to cheaper photography and computerized graphic design for their poster art. The arrival of large-format printers into Thailand in the early 1990s had a chilling effect on the movie billboard painters. Theatre owners, already feeling the squeeze of declining ticket sales, began changing over to the much cheaper machines. One by one, theatres made the switch, laying waste to an entire guild once widespread and deeply admired. It was a textbook case of machine making obsolescence of man.

In the larger Thai cities, LED screens have become the new norm for roadside movie ads, the single most effective (and intrusive) way of drawing the eye of the passerby. In Bangkok, the epicentre of Thailand's film industry, there are currently no active movie billboard painters. At one time indispensable to the marketing of

films, this craft has dwindled down to a bare-bones number of active artists across the country and there are now only a few independent theatres across Thailand that eschew the blinding commercialism of LED in favour of the soft stroke of a painter. As of this writing, the Colosseum Cineplex keeps a lone studio employed in the town of Yala and the MVP Cineplex in Sisaket still has a painter doing its movie ads, as does the Five Star Cineplex in Nakhon Ratchasima.

Thanks to the foresight of collectors, many of the posters painted during the heyday of Thailand's movie poster and billboard art have been carefully preserved for posterity. Thai posters from the 1960s through the '80s are now coveted among movie poster aficionados the world over, with a number of the artists who created them having quietly attained cult status. The following pages show some highlights from the author's own collection.

ดิโน เดอ ลอเรนติส
เสนอ.
ชาร์ล บรอนสัน เป็น...
นักล่าชาติหิน
"DEATH WISH"
สีเทคนิค
ฉายที่
โปรดเลือก พรรคกิจสังคม เพื่อให้ชาติบ้านเมืองร่มเย็นเป็นสุข
วันที่

**Men of Stone and Steel:** *Charles Bronson movies were wildly popular in Thai theatres during the 1960s and '70s. Because of the often stoic tough-guy roles he played, Thai distributors gave Bronson the informal title of Chat Hin (roughly translating as Stone Cold). Other famous action stars were given similar titular treatment. Arnold Schwarzenegger became known as Khon Lek (Steel Man) and Chuck Norris was known as Diao (The One). All three of the posters pictured here were designed and painted by Tongdee Panumas.*

วันประวัติศาสตร์
ของ ไทย-จีน
ท่านจะได้ชมความเร้นลับมหัศจรรย์
ที่ถูกปิดกว่า 50 ปีของ "ยักษ์หลับแห่งเอเชีย"
โดยยกกองถ่ายทั่วทิเบต หลายสิบคน

**Cold War Diplomacy on the Big Screen:** *When Thai Prime Minister Kukrit Pramoj travelled to Peking (now Beijing), China, in 1975 to establish formal diplomatic relations with Mao Zedong's China, a camera crew came along to document the historic event. The footage was edited into a documentary film called* 7 Wan Nai Peking (7 Days in Peking) *and shown in Thai theatres.*

King Kong, 1977 (painted by Tongdee Panumas).

**King Kongfusion:** In 1977, a remake of the cinema classic King Kong was released in theatres around the world. As Thai theatres were preparing for this cinema event, one distribution company re-released the original 1933 version (directed by Merian C. Cooper and Ernest B. Schoedsack) hoping to profit off the hype from the soon-to-be-released new version. Chawana Boonchu was commissioned to do the artwork, which depicts King Kong on top of the Empire State Building as in the original film. Tongdee Panumas was commissioned to do the artwork for the new version (left), which shows the king of apes straddling the World Trade Center towers. Shortly after its re-release, the original King Kong was pulled from theatres, along with the stunning new poster, on the grounds that it was misleading viewers who believed they were going to see the new version. As a result, the poster painted by Chawana Boonchu is extremely rare.

King Kong, 1933 *(painted by Chawana Boonchu to coincide with the 1977 remake).*

**Violent Colours:** *Kampol Niyomthai, or Kham as he signed his artwork, was the go-to artist for Chinese-language films that entered the Thai market in the 1970s and '80s. His colourful palette gave posters for one of the most action-packed film genres a bright, playful air even if the content was anything but. Case in point: the dazzling orange hues employed by Kham for Polly Shang Kwan's Heroine of Tribulation (1981), underscoring a foreground depicting brutal violence.*

**Neo-Noir Artistry:** *This exquisite poster for the French crime thriller directed by Jean Reno was painted by Tongdee Panumas. As with many Thai posters for foreign films, the artwork for Nikita, 1990, (also called* La Femme Nikita) *was a partial simulacrum of the poster from its country of origin. The birds-eye view of the street was copied from the original French poster and then combined with the central figure of actress Ann Parillaud from the film's American poster. In typical Thai poster fashion, Tongdee added a tantalizing array of vignettes and visages using a neo-noir colour palette.*

189

# EPILOGUE

When my plan to document Thailand's standalone movie theatres was first hatched back in 2008, it was unimaginable that the country's entire collection would be on the verge of extinction just ten years later. At the time of this writing, there are a grand total of three active standalone movie theatres nationwide, down from approximately 25 when I began documenting them. These are the Scala (page 100), Det Udom Mini (page 141) and Chum Phae Cineplex (page 142); while the Sala Chalerm Krung (page 26) retains film exhibition capabilities it is primarily programmed with stage events. If we include a smattering of 'cruising' theatres that have managed to stay in business across Bangkok – more likely due to owners waiting for the land value to rise than to any concerted commitment to the theatre itself – then there are approximately eight active standalone movie theatres in the entire country.

While it is true in general that standalone theatres have suffered similar fates throughout the world – usually for the same techno-evolutionary reasons that they have in Thailand – perhaps in no other country has their decline been so all-encompassing. This is partly due to the fact that Thailand's two nationwide theatre chains have coupled all their branches with either car-centric shopping malls or, in the case of Bangkok, transit-oriented developments. In short, they have wisely noted that accessibility lies in the convenience of parking for a country that has fallen deeply in love with the combustion engine. Furthermore, since at least the 1990s, the age demographics of movie-going in Thailand has dropped drastically. Teens and twenty-somethings have become the dominant market, and climate-controlled shopping malls make excellent hang-outs for them. A spate of theatre closings between 2015 and 2018 can be attributed to yet another factor; a single traumatic change within the film exhibition industry. Namely, the switch from analogue film to digital projection. Once distributors stopped supplying theatres with traditional 35 mm film prints, theatre owners were forced to make the costly investment in digital projection systems or close their doors. In the face of all-time low viewership, most reluctantly chose the latter.

Between the traditional standalone theatre and the contemporary multiplex, a handful of cinemas have popped up over the years that embody the community spirit of old. Most of them, including the Friese-Greene Club, Bangkok Screening Room and Cinema Oasis, were carved out of existing shop-houses in Bangkok. Along with House RCA (which will soon be changing locations) all do a stand-up job of bringing unique programming to the city's cinephile community. Outside of Bangkok, however, these types of venues are sorely lacking.

Despite these broader trends away from the standalone model of movie theatres, there have been a few efforts to preserve them in Thailand. Aside from the well-known Sala Chalerm Krung, which survives by hosting live *khon* classical theatre performances, there are two other cases worth mentioning: namely, the Scala and the Sala Chalerm Thani, also known as the Nang Loeng (page 22). In 2016, the Thai Film Archive developed a master plan for preserving the now 100-year-old Sala Chalerm Thani theatre, possibly the oldest existing purpose-built movie theatre in Southeast Asia. The plan calls for the theatre to be restored as a living museum and community cultural centre with working cinema functions included. By early 2019, renovations by the Crown Property Bureau, which owns the land, had commenced. Scala, on the other hand, currently lacks a master plan for preservation, despite the fact that its contract with landlord Chulalongkorn University is set to expire in 2020. Hope for a functional long-term future lies exclusively in its wide popular support, which will ensure the university due recognition as steward of Bangkok's cinema heritage if heeded.

If the renovation of either of these theatres proves successful, or should any of the other rumoured theatre renovations come to fruition, it is possible that other locations in Thailand will take inspiration and bring their old standalone movie theatres back to life. As the trend towards smart urbanism, historic preservation and sustainable living continues to grow in fits and starts around the world, it seems possible that at least some of Thailand's old theatres may find a new lease of life.

Manop, former projectionist at the Bang Pa-In Rama theatre, pictured at his old work station wearing the motorcycle taxi driver's vest he donned after losing his job when the theatre closed in 1996.

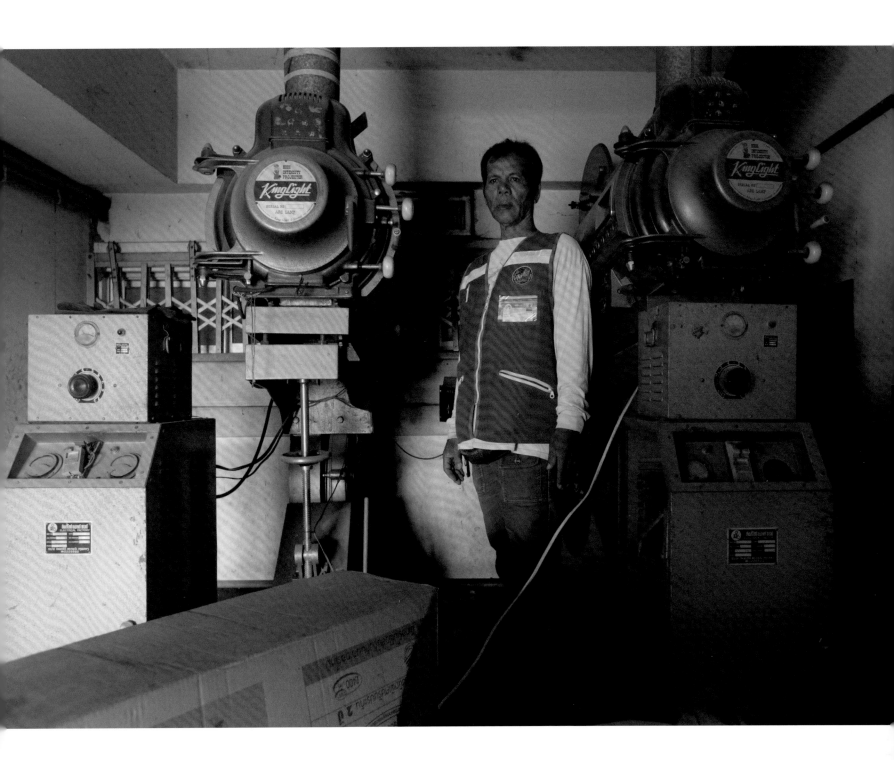

# ACKNOWLEDGEMENTS

This project may very well have fizzled out within a year had it not been for the assistance, encouragement and time of numerous individuals, including but not limited to the following:

Bill and Eric Booth, and Gridthiya Gaweewong of the Jim Thompson Foundation, who from the fledgling days of this project saw its inherent historical value. Dr. Chayan Vaddhanaphuti, my academic adviser and mentor at Chiang Mai University, who strayed from tradition to allow Thailand's movie theatres to become a thesis topic. Dr. Dome Sukwong, Chalida Uabumrungjit and Sanchai Chotirosseranee of the Thai Film Archive for providing a historical foundation from which to examine Thailand's movie theatres, as well as for giving me a much-needed boost several years into the project.

Furthermore, I owe a debt of gratitude to Rebecca Weldon for her ceaseless encouragement over the years; to Tom Van Blarcom for further encouragement, support and friendship; and to Nicholas Simon for more of the same, as well as providing a comfortable and culturally enriching environment when working in Bangkok.

Over the past year, I have gained great insights from my many conversations with Toh Panthamit, whose lifetime in the movie business has proven to be a wellspring of valuable information.

A huge thanks to River Books, my publishing house, specifically Narisa Chakrabongse and Paisarn Piemmettawat, who patiently bore with me through many delays and hiccups in order to bring this book to fruition. And to the editorial/design team, Sarah Rooney and Ruetairat (Fon) Nanta, for making the most gruelling part of the book-making process a delight.

Lastly, many thanks to the numerous theatre owners, employees and movie-goers of Thailand who gave me the time of day and access to their movie theatre memories. Their stories helped me understand this facet of leisure in Thailand's past and brought to life the pages of this book.

Corridor at the Kitti Rama theatre, Chachoengsao.

INDEX TO
MOVIE THEATRES

# THAILAND

**Ayutthaya**
Bang Pa-In Rama (1981), 87

**Bangkok**
Bang Khae Rama (1971), 113
Lido theatre (1968), 96
Mongkol Rama (1963), 112
Nakhon Non Rama (1982), 115
Prince theatre (1912), 21
Sala Chalerm Krung (1933), 26
Sala Chalerm Thani, also Nang Loeng (1918), 22
Scala theatre (1969), 100
Siam theatre (1966), 93
Thonburi Rama (1972), 114

**Chachoengsao**
Siri Phanom Rama (1978), 74

**Chanthaburi**
Chanthaburi Multiplex (1980), 73

**Chiang Mai**
Khemsawat Theatre (1975), 46

**Kalasin**
Somdet theatre (1981), 61
Prince Cineplex (1972), 138

**Khon Kaen**
Chum Phae Cineplex (2001), 142

**Lampang**
Sri Nakhon theatre (1957), 41

**Loei**
Amarin theatre (1978), 58

**Lopburi**
Thahan Bok theatre (1941), 32

**Nan**
Pua Rama theatre (1979), 64

**Nakhon Pathom**
Kamphaeng Saen Rama (1982), 88

**Nakhon Ratchasima**
Chalerm Por theatre (1957), 50
Sri Pong Cineplex (2005), 143

**Nakhon Sawan**
Wathana theatre (1961), 44

**Nong Khai**
Thepbanterng theatre (1971), 57

**Pattani**
Paradise theatre (1981), 133

**Phayao**
Phayao Rama (1958), 42

**Prachuab Khiri Khan**
Bang Saphan Noi (1981), 124
Pranburi Rama (c.1980), 123

**Ratchaburi**
Chalerm Thongkham (1958), 120
Khosit theatre (1983), 127
Wik Kru Thawee theatre (1958), 118

**Rayong**
Burapha theatre (1974), 69

**Sa Kaeo**
Sa Kaeo Rama (1983), 77

**Samut Sakhon**
Mahachai Rama (1972), 82

**Singburi**
Mueang Thong Rama (1969), 81

**Songkhla**
Saha theatre (1929), 24

**Sukhothai**
Ma Win Rama (1972), 45
Amarin Rama (1976), 47

**Suphanburi**
Fah Siam (1972), 85

**Trat**
Dara theatre (mid-1970s), 66

**Trang**
Petch Rama (1978), 132

**Ubon Ratchathani**
Det Udom Mini theatre (1990), 141

**Udon Thani**
Vista theatre (1967), 54

**Uthai Thani**
New Chalerm Uthai theatre (1943), 34

**Yala**
Luna theatre (1960), 130
Siam theatre (1961), 131

# LAOS

**Luang Prabang**
Sien Savan theatre (1962), 153

**Oudomxay**
The Lao-Viet Cultural Hall of Friendship (1981), 159

**Savannakhet**
Lao Chaleun theatre (c. 1930s), 149
Nang Lit theatre (c. 1970), 156
Seno Rama theatre (1970), 154

**Vientiane**
Vieng Samay theatre (1957), 151

The Mongkol Rama theatre, Kanchanaburi.

(Please check your personal belongings
before leaving your seat.)